# Biorhythms

## IS THIS YOUR DAY?

# Biorhythms

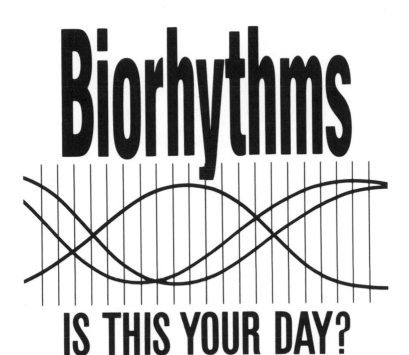

# IS THIS YOUR DAY?

## HOW YOU CAN CHART YOUR UPS AND DOWNS FOR WEEKS, MONTHS, AND EVEN YEARS AHEAD

GEORGE S. THOMMEN

Crown Publishers, Inc.
New York

Published by Crown Publishers, Inc., 225 Park Avenue South, New York, New York 10003, and represented in Canada by the Canadian MANDA Group

CROWN is a trademark of Crown Publishers, Inc.

Manufactured in the United States of America

Library of Congress Cataloging-in-Publication Data
Thommen, George S., 1896-
  Biorhythms: is this your day?

  Reprint. Originally published: Is this your day? New York : Crown, 1973.
  Bibliography: p.
  1. Biological rhythms.   I. Title
QP84.6.T46 1986      612'.022      86-8971
ISBN 0-517-56244-8
10 9 8 7 6 5 4 3 2 1
First Revised Edition

*The author wishes to express his appreciation
to May W. Lamont for her help
in the research and composition for this
new edition.*

# CONTENTS

*vii*

# FOREWORD

The subject of this book is people. In the pages that follow, you will
find references to mathematics, cell structure, accidents, human error, heart attacks, sports events, births, sex-determination, marital·
compatibility, and even missile shots into outer space. But the common denominator throughout these pages is man, and how he feels,
acts, and thinks. The scope of this book may seem quite broad, but
that is only because man himself lives such a varied life.

This book tries to answer a question I first asked myself many
years ago. It's a rather simple question, which I believe everyone
has asked: "Why do I feel different today from the way I felt yester-
day, or last week or last month?" For centuries we have been con-
tent to say that man, as well as woman, is a fickle creature and that
his moods, attitudes, thoughts, abilities, and actions change from
day to day. The common greeting, "How are you, today?" is simply a recognition that we change with time, like everything else in
the universe.

As man progressed through the ages, his ability to question
also made advances. At the beginning of this century, a number of
thinking men began to probe further into the question of why man's
disposition differs from day to day. Perhaps because these men were
psychoanalysts and medical doctors, they considered themselves
closer to the question of human behavior and feeling. The vogue of
applying reason and logic to the natural sciences attracted the attention of the scientists of the period, for it seemed to hold some prom-
ise of helping to solve this problem. In other cases, the application
of such ordered disciplines as mathematics seemed only to confuse

and muddle the progress that had been made in the search for a clear-cut order in complicated areas of human knowledge. But, hopefully enough, there seemed to be some down-to-earth evidence to indicate that man's existence might, like many other pieces in nature's puzzle, have an orderly basis that would yield to logical analysis and insight.

The application of mathematics to the biological scheme of things was called biorhythm. More literally, we can think of this science as bio-mathematics. The principle, however, is clear: nature is ordered; order can be analyzed by mathematics; therefore, insight into nature, and particularly into the human being, can be secured by using mathematics as a probe, a tool to explore human activity.

Mathematics is used in this sense as an aid or guide rather than a rule or prediction of behavior and experience. Often I have found the evidence supporting the rhythmic theory overwhelming. I mention this, not to assert that what I will say in the following pages should be unquestionably accepted—that is only for the reader to decide—but to suggest that this is how I myself became familiar with the subject.

Some of the propositions advanced to the reader in later pages may seem, quite frankly, unreasonable and overstated. The point is that when I was introduced to biorhythm, these same arguments appeared just as incredible to me. Because of this, I ask of the reader one indulgence: *to read this book with an open mind* and explore to his own satisfaction the reasoning and evidence presented. To this end I have included calculation tables, the three cycle rulers, and chart blanks. These charting aids will allow the reader to evaluate the reasoning and evidence presented, to expose the validity of biorhythm mathematics to his own experience, to discuss it with friends, and to submit it to any "test" of his own devising.

I ask the reader's indulgence because that is the way I came to know the value of biorhythm in my own life. This book can tell and explain only what we already know; it is up to the reader to perform the difficult task of evaluating what he reads. I hope your experience will be as fulfilling as mine.

George S. Thommen

"By the Law of Periodical Repetition, everything which has happened once must happen again and again—and not capriciously, but at regular periods, and each thing in its own period, not another's, and each obeying its own law . . . the same Nature which delights in periodical repetition in the skies is the Nature which orders the affairs of the earth. Let us not underrate the value of that hint."

—MARK TWAIN

# FINDING THE RHYTHMS OF LIFE

## DR. HERMANN SWOBODA, PSYCHOLOGIST

Man is known as the curious animal; it has been said that his curiosity sets him apart from the beast. It is not difficult to understand why one of the favorite targets of this curiosity is man's own behavior, the examination of the scope and variety of his own actions, thoughts, and feelings. One of the most interesting things man has found out by looking at himself is how each individual can differ from all others. An equally interesting observation is how different a single individual can be at different times.

Everyone experiences days when everything he does seems to be right and, on the other hand, days which nothing he does seems to make any sense. This state of affairs is not new; man has long puzzled over the range of his own actions and feelings. Even Hippocrates, the traditional physician's physician, advised his students and associates some 2,400 years ago to observe the "good" and "bad" days among the healthy and the ill, and to take these fluctuations into consideration in the treatment of patients.

Although man understood that he acted, felt, and thought differently at different times, for centuries a fundamental question went unanswered, even unasked. At the end of the nineteenth century, Dr. Hermann Swoboda, professor of psychology at the University of Vienna, was prompted by his research findings to wonder whether there might not be some regularity or rhythm to these fundamental changes in man's disposition. Swoboda apparently was impressed by John Beard's report of 1897 on the span of gestation and the cycle of birth, and by the publication of a scientific paper on bisexuality in man by Wilhelm Fliess. He was also keenly interested in the observations made by the philosopher Johann Friedrich Herbart on *Freisteigende Vorstellungen.*[1] However, Herbart had not found a law of regularity.

Swoboda, in his first report, presented at the University of Vienna at the turn of the century, noted:

> One does not need to have lived a long span of life before one comes to realize that life is subject to consistent changes. This realization is not a reflection on the changes in our fate or the changes which take place during various stages of life. Even if someone could live a life completely devoid of outside influences, a life during which nothing whatever disturbs the mental or physical aspect, life would nevertheless *not* be the same day after day. The best of health does not prevent man from feeling unwell at times, or less cheerful than he is normally.

During his initial research between 1897 and 1902, Swoboda recorded the recurrence of pain and the swelling of tissues such as is experienced in insect bites. He discovered a periodicity in fevers, in the outbreak of an illness, and in heart attacks, a phenomenon Fliess had reported in a medical review, which led to the discovery of certain basic rhythms in man—one a 23-day cycle and the other a 28-day cycle.

However, Swoboda, as a psychologist, was mainly interested in finding out whether man's feelings and actions were influenced by rhythmical fluctuations and whether these rhythms could be precalculated. The results of his persistent research can be summed up in his own words:

---

[1] All publications marked with an asterisk (*) are listed in the Bibliography, where complete publishing information is given.

We will no longer ask *why* man acts one way or another, because we have learned to recognize that his action is influenced by periodic changes and that man's reaction to an impression can be foreseen, or predicted, to use a stronger term. Such a psychoanalysis could be called *bionomy* because, as in chemistry where the researcher can anticipate the outcome of a formula, through bionomy the psychologist can anticipate, or predict, so to speak, the periodic changes in man.

Swoboda was an analytical thinker and a systematic recorder. His painstaking research in psychology and periodicity produced convincing evidence of rhythms in life. He showed a deep interest in the study of dreams and their origin, and noted that melodies and ideas would often repeat in one's mind after periodic intervals, generally based on a 23-day or a 28-day rhythm. In searching for the origin of these rhythms, Swoboda carefully noted the birth of infants among his patients and found that young mothers would often have anxious hours about the health of their babies during periodic days after birth. He reasoned that this phenomenon, which was often accompanied by the infant's refusal to take nourishment, was a sign of rhythmical development; on these days the tempo of digestion and absorption was apparently slower. He advised the mothers not to worry, since these periodic crises could be considered part of natural development and growth. Similar rhythmical turning points were reported in asthma attacks.

Swoboda's first book was *Die Perioden des Menschlichen Lebens* (The Periodicity in Man's Life).* This book was followed by his *Studien zur Grundlegung der Psychologie* (Studies of the Basis of Psychology).* In order to facilitate his research and also to encourage other scientists and medical doctors in the recording of the mathematical rhythms, Swoboda designed a slide rule with which it was fairly simple to find the "critical" days in the life of any person whose birth date was known. The instruction booklet was entitled *Die Kritischen Tage des Menschen* (The Critical Days of Man).*

I had the pleasure and honor of corresponding with Dr. Swoboda until he died in June, 1963. He was ninety years old at his

*Fig. 1:* Dr. Hermann Swoboda, Vienna, 1873–1963.

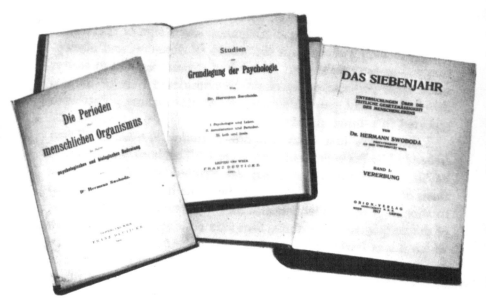

*Fig. 2:* Three of the original books by Dr. Swoboda in which the 23-day and the 28-day rhythms of life were first explained and documented with hundreds of examples.

4

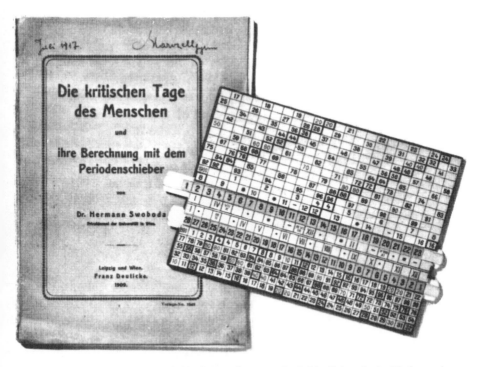

*Fig. 3:* The slide rule Dr. Swoboda designed to trace the "critical" days in the 23-day and 28-day life rhythms for any birth date. The instruction book explains the application and the method of calculation.

death, but even during the last years of his life his keen interest in biorhythm prevailed. Available to me are the notes he left with his family and with his old friend, Dr. Arthur Dietrich, which include his slide rule and instruction booklet, as well as books and the lectures he presented at the University of Vienna and over the Vienna radio network. Among these papers is a fundamental study of rhythmical development in cancer, which may yet attract the attention of cancer researchers. Swoboda was awarded a special honor medal by the city of Vienna for his life work in the study of psychology and the rhythms in life, and in 1951 the University of Vienna renewed his professorship and gave him an additional honorary degree.

His most profound work was a 576-page volume entitled *Das Siebenjahr* (The Year of Seven),* which contains the 23-day and

28-day mathematical analysis of the rhythmical repetition of births through generations. With documentation covering hundreds of family trees, he endeavored to verify that most major events in life, such as birth, the onset of an illness, heart attacks, and death, fall on periodic days and involve family relationships.

In one of his letters, Dr. Swoboda indicated that eight trunks of research documentation that he had stored in the vaults of the University of Vienna fell into the hands of Russian troops during the occupation of Vienna in 1945. This loss was a bitter blow to Swoboda.

## WILHELM FLIESS, M.D.

*His Discovery of Rhythms in Man*

The amazing fact is that while Swoboda was concentrating his studies of the rhythms in life and in man on observations in the field of psychology, some three hundred miles away in Berlin a practicing physician, Wilhelm Fliess, was accumulating a vast amount of research material in order to confirm 23-day and 28-day rhythms he had observed while diagnosing many of his patients. Fliess was a nose and throat specialist, but the breadth of his medical and biological interest was far-reaching. He showed great knowledge in many fields of science, and records indicate that he was elected president of the Germanic Academy of Sciences in 1910. Fliess enjoyed a large and prosperous practice in Berlin and lectured extensively. His research led him to reason that a periodic process must affect both man and woman and that these rhythms could be traced throughout life. Believing that each individual inherits both male and female sexual characteristics, he concluded that everyone has elements of bisexuality in his makeup. He also concluded that there was a connection between the rhythms he had observed and evolution, the creation of organisms, and life itself.

A review of the lectures and medical reports Fliess published between 1895 and 1905 shows that he was anxious to find out why some children, exposed to a contagious disease, would remain immune for days, only to succumb on a periodic day. By tracing illnesses, the outbreak of fevers, and deaths back to birth, Fliess became convinced that a 23-day and a 28-day rhythm was fundamental to life.

Fliess recorded his discoveries of 23-day and 28-day rhythms in his book *Der Ablauf Des Lebens* (The Course of Life),* a 564-page volume with which he expected to arouse the interest of the medical profession. He was disappointed. Reviewers reported that although the work contained a vast amount of mathematical research and statistics, it only confused the reader. A critic conceded: "Fliess shows an astoundingly varied knowledge of medicine, mathematics, genealogy, botany, zoology, astrology, and psychology." Three additional books, containing further documentation and reprints of the lectures Fliess had presented at numerous medical and scientific meetings, were published between 1909 and 1925 under the titles *Vom Leben und Vom Tod* (Of Life and Death),* *Das Jahr im Lebendigen* (The Year in the Living),* *Zur Periodenlehre* (The Theory of Periodicity),* a collection of lectures.

Fliess was assisted in his research by a mathematician, and subsequently by Hans Schlieper, another medical doctor who produced his own works on the subject of rhythms in life under the titles *Der Rhythmus im Lebendigen* (Periodicity of Life),* and *Das Jahr im Raum* (The Year in Space) *

In his research into rhythmical repetition in life, Fliess also studied inherited characteristics, especially left-handedness, which he ascribed to a greater influence of the sensitivity (feminine) rhythm reflecting a higher degree of creative feelings such as is often observed in artists, composers, and writers. He recorded births and deaths in connection with family tree studies and established a mathematical connection in blood relationship going back over many generations. Sensing that nature seemed to have given a "clock" to many of her children, Fliess continued exploring the regular patterns affecting all phases of life. He concluded that the 23-day (masculine) rhythm affected the physical condition of man.

7

## The Second Life Rhythm

The second long-term rhythm, this one of 28-day duration, was ascribed by Fliess to the rhythmical changes of the feminine inheritance. Originating in the nervous system or fibers, it influences the emotions and one's degree of sensitivity. Fliess, a thorough researcher, explained his theories with firm conviction and documented them with an impressive collection of statistical data, tracing the origin of the rhythms back to birth. His revelations, to say the least, caused a good deal of controversy among his colleagues. They accepted the fact that man's physical makeup and his emotions are continually changing; but it was, understandably, difficult for them to take the next step and agree that these changes were influenced not only by what man experienced in his everyday living, but—quite fundamentally—by his very biological constitution. To Fliess, it seemed as if nature had given man a master clock in addition to the more obvious rhythms that pulse throughout the animal and plant kingdom. There are, of course, innumerable examples of precise rhythms in all forms of life, from the simplest virus to the most complicated creatures.

The real problem, it soon became clear, was not discovering the master clock—Fliess had most of the right answers in that respect—but convincing man that the master clock literally beating inside his own body actually did tick off the measure of his life. It was just a bit too tempting to throw out all this "biological mathematics" and say that, after all, man might be conceived and born under nature's laws, but there was no reason why he had to live under them.

In a book published in 1942, George Riebold, a gynecologist, reviewed the fundamental ideas developed by Fliess between 1908 and 1928. Riebold said that "some truth lurks in the idea that life follows a periodic rhythm . . . and that the periods of 23 days and 28 days which Fliess discovered are of frequent occurrence." Some of the discoveries, he reported, had been adopted into modern concepts of gynecology and otolaryngology.

The evidence presented in the balance of this book attempts to demonstrate that man, far from being burdened by his biological

*Fig. 4:* Wilhelm Fliess, M.D., Berlin, 1859–1928.

*Fig. 5:* The original books by Wilheim Fliess, M.D., and his associate Hans Schlieper, M.D., documenting and explaining the discovery of a 23-day and a 28-day rhythm in man.

heritage, can live a richer life by understanding and making use of nature's endowments.

## Biorhythm and Sigmund Freud

The word *biorhythm* has a logical enough derivation. It is simply a compound of the common Greek term for life, *bios,* and another word borrowed from the Greek, *rhythmos,* which indicates a regulated beat and is generally associated with such arts as music and poetry. The *rhythm* in *biorhythm* is used in the same sense, a regulated beat, and just as in music and poetry, we find a definite, precise method of calculating and applying this rhythm. We might even say, to carry the example farther, that Nature is the composer; man, as a human being, is the instrument upon which Nature plays her rhapsodies; man, as a scientist, is the listener, trying to appreciate, to fathom and comprehend the simple elegance and beauty of the composition.

Analyzing Nature's tunes was a popular effort during the end of the last century in such European countries as Austria, Germany, France, Switzerland, and Belgium. It was in these countries that the basic principles of biorhythm were first developed and explored. The evidence that first suggested rhythms really exist in man is familiar enough to anyone who has visited a doctor's office and seen charts of body temperatures, respiration rates, blood pressure, and other measurable manifestations of the body.

The word *rhythm* is also used in reference to the menstrual cycle in woman, for which a 28-day periodicity is the apparent average. Two questions were foremost in the mind of original researchers: First, why does this supposedly regular menstrual rhythm vary in length in different women (and even in the same woman) from about 26 to 35 days? Secondly, why should woman alone be subject to rhythmical development? Is not man also, the researchers reasoned, the combination and offspring of both male and female cell development?

After Fliess had reported on bisexuality in man, he observed a 23-day rhythmical repetition in fevers and recurrent illness in some of his patients. This led him to believe that both a 23-day and 28-day rhythm affected the regularity of the menstrual rhythm and that all life is influenced by these two long-term rhythms. Through evolution, he reasoned, man and woman have inherited bisexuality and therefore are influenced by both rhythms. The breast nipples on the male are only one of the numerous physical marks left as reminders of man's dual sex evolution.

Fliess, a contemporary and close friend of Sigmund Freud, studied medicine at the University of Berlin, where he was graduated about 1885. In medical literature Fliess is referred to as *Sanitaetsrat,* which is the modern-day equivalent of a member of the Board of Health of Berlin. His discovery of bisexuality and his observation of rhythmic cycles in the phenomena of births, illness, behavior, and death were frequent subjects of discussion between him and Freud. Medical history has evidence to show that Fliess's theories were of great interest and importance to Freud during his early work in developing his psychoanalytical concepts. Correspondence referring to their discussions between 1887 and 1902 (consisting of 184 letters written by Freud to Fliess) was collected by Freud's daughter Anna and her friend Princess Marie Bonaparte. These letters were translated into English by Eric Mosbacher and James Strachey under the title *The Origin of Psychoanalysis, Sigmund Freud's Letters.*[2] Unfortunately, the letters from Fliess to Freud were not included, and so this presentation is rather one-sided. My own investigation revealed that most of the books and documentation left by Fliess after his death in 1928 were destroyed during World War II.

In January, 1959, *Prevention Magazine* carried a reprint of a pertinent article from the *Eye, Ear, Nose and Throat Monthly,* en titled "Sigmund Freud's Otolaryngological Ordeal," by Noah D. Fabricant, M.D. Fabricant noted that "in the period between 1887 and 1902 Freud formed a close friendship with Wilhelm Fliess, a Berlin nose and throat specialist whose medical knowledge and scientific interests extended over an area far wider than his comparatively restricted field." Fliess performed two operations on Freud, and warned his friend strongly against excessive smoking and the danger of inducing cancer of the throat. When death claimed Freud, it was reported to have been caused by cancer of the throat.

---

[2] Basic Books, New York, 1954.

What is apparent, from this review and from the material published in the book *The Origin of Psychoanalysis,* is Freud's early struggles for recognition and his agreement with many of Fliess's analyses. The two, however, were far apart in their economic status. Although Fliess enjoyed a prominent role in the German Scientific Society and was a successful and prosperous surgeon in Berlin, Freud was barely able to provide enough comfort for his growing family in Vienna.

There is a lesson to be learned from the lifetime efforts of the pioneers in biorhythm, Swoboda and Fliess. It is included in these pages because it is important to an understanding of the history of biorhythm, or, for that matter, of just about any new idea that stretches the imagination of man beyond his common experience. Fliess was primarily a researcher in the field of life rhythms. In their questioning, however, both Swoboda and Fliess felt that the problem of rhythms in nature could best be solved by examining as many facets of her manifestations as possible. Independently, both studied family trees, hoping to find out why births often followed a rhythmic family pattern. Curiosity led them to attempt to establish a biological pattern between siblings, and between the child and his parents and grandparents. They were curious to know how the single egg cell, the ovum, after being fertilized by the sperm cell, could multiply astronomically and after only about thirty cell divisions could reach the comparative perfection of the human organism and eventually result in a strikingly accurate reproduction of the parent.

Their awe of nature led these pioneers to experiment with numbers as a tool in deciphering her wondrous accomplishments. The irony of their quest was that this very use of mathematics helped largely to defeat their attempts to gain wide acceptance for the very conclusions that mathematics helped them to reach. By applying numbers to the realm of man and medicine, Fliess had come up with concepts that were daring, original, and—most important—seemingly quite valid. Yet by burdening his published works with these encumbrances—pages and pages of numerical tables, charts, calculations, and proofs—he frightened the medical profession as well as the public he sought to convince. His critics said his presentation was too complex. His readers were either unable or unwilling to wade through the multitude of statistics, and although no one could disprove his mathematical calculations, it might have appeared that they almost discouraged analysis. Unable to communicate his own ideas effectively, Fliess was never to achieve the fame of other scientists who were more fortunate in overcoming the indifference they encountered when trying to explain the powerful relationship between biology and mathematics.


*The Rhythm of the Mind*

What has made the study of biorhythm such a fascinating experience is the fact that pieces of supporting evidence were discovered by researchers who not only did not know each other but were not even aware of the work previously done in the science. Yet results have been remarkably consistent and encouraging, and new directions and dimensions have continued to be added to the established principles. So, in a very real way, it was with biorhythm's third major precept: the cycle of the mind.

During the 1920's Alfred Teltscher, a doctor of engineering and a teacher, reportedly collected a large number of performance reports of high school and college students at Innsbruck. Himself a student of nature as well as of mathematics, Teltscher wondered why the intellectual capability of students seemed to vary from time to time, and whether any exact pattern could be established. Unfortunately, my own search abroad brought to light no original documentation, scientific paper, or book of his, and so my knowledge of Teltscher's work is based on secondhand reports and on articles that discussed his findings.

Apparently, even the comparatively limited basis of his statistical sampling disclosed that an exact pattern could be established. The paper Teltscher supposedly prepared concluded that the students' high and low peaks of performance fluctuated in a definite 33-day cycle. He stated, in effect, that there were periods during which a student could readily grasp and absorb new subjects, and, on the other hand, there were comparable periods during which the capacity to think quickly and clearly was diminished. His associates and medical contemporaries ascribed this rhythm to periodic secretions of glands affecting the brain cells, possibly of the thyroid gland.

On the other side of the Atlantic Ocean, meanwhile, Dr. Rexford Hersey at the University of Pennsylvania, assisted by Dr. Michael John Bennett, conducted a similar research between 1928 and 1932. Hersey reported the accidental discovery of a 33-day to 36-day rhythm, revealed by checking the emotions of workers in railroad shops over periods of many months. His findings were published in his book *Workers' Emotions in Shop and Home.*

Donald A. Laird, director of the psychological laboratory at Colgate University, reviewed Hersey's discovery in an article that appeared in *Review of Reviews*, April, 1935, entitled "The Secrets of Our Ups and Downs," and was reprinted in *Reader's Digest*, August, 1935. At the conclusion Laird declared:

> To most people moods are an eternal puzzle, no one knows whence they come or where they go. Science has recently discovered moods are by no means matters of chance. They are not, as we have long supposed, simply reactions to the success or failure of our plans. On the contrary, they grow within us as a direct result of the rise and fall of our emotional energy. It has been proved that our bodies and minds produce, store up and spend our emotional energy in regular cycles.

Laird's comments, although widely read, failed to capture the imagination of the public or the medical profession.

A similar attempt was made a decade later by Myron Stearns, who, writing for *Redbook* in November, 1945, under the title "Do You Know Your Emotional Cycles?" tried to stir up some attention for the science. A month later, *Reader's Digest* picked up the *Redbook* article.

Stearns quoted Hersey as having said: "Few people paid any attention to my book, except some far-sighted officials of the Pennsylvania Railroad Company, who supported my work from the beginning." Hersey was also quoted as remarking that "everybody knows we have ups and downs, but we don't know what causes them."

Hersey produced another book on cyclical behavior, published by Harper and Brothers in 1955 under the title *Zest for Work*. The material used in this volume was based on the reports of a number of workers who volunteered to keep their own records on how they reacted and what they said. In the last chapter some attempt was made to correlate the cyclical emotional changes with organic functions.

In the book *Biorhythm, A Scientific Exploration into the Life Cycles of the Individual,* * by Hans Wernli, the account of Dr. Fliess's discovery of biorhythm is narrated. The book also delves into the meaning of the theory and into its relation to man's daily life—the influence of both the low and high phases of the cycles. It explains, too, how biorhythm can be applied to various situations and jobs and gives complete details of the procedure for computing biorhythms.

In summing up the medical aspect and value of biorhythm, Dr. F. Wehrli of Locarno, Switzerland, wrote: "There is no doubt that applied biorhythm can bring many benefits to everyday life. It will enable the individual to meet responsibilities in a better way and to improve his physical, emotional and intellectual achievements."

# 2

# CALCULATING THE RHYTHMS OF LIFE

Until the late 1930's, the tedious and time-consuming calculations necessary for figuring out the correct position of each of the three rhythms for any particular day was rather involved. Those interested in biorhythm studies had to produce their charts or records by a complicated series of computations, unless they were able to obtain one of the slide rules designed by Swoboda in 1909. Perhaps the slow procedure was one of the reasons why biorhythm did not gain broad acceptance, although the book by Fliess did contain numerous tables in a cumbersome attempt to facilitate the calculations.

Biorhythm's limitations in this respect were recognized by Alfred Judt of Bremen, Germany, during the late 1920's. As a doctor of engineering and a mathematician by profession, Judt's primary interest at first was studying the variations in the performances of sports figures. So that he could quickly compute the rhythm position of an athlete, he designed calculation tables establishing a relationship between the day of birth, the year of birth, and the day of a sports event. Between 1929 and 1934, Judt published his research in two books with the titles: *Biologische Rhythmen und Sportsleistung* (Biological Rhythms and Performances in Sports), and *Arzt und Periodenlehre* (The Medical Doctor and the Theory of Periodicity).

During the same period of years, the Swiss engineer and mathematician Hans R. Frueh became interested in biorhythm mathematics, and studied the available records and books. To facilitate carrying on his own research, he perfected the calculation tables originated by Judt. Later, he designed a hand-operated calculator

*16*

into which the tables were built. One side showed the calculation tables, and the other side the respective setting for the current month.

## REVIEW OF RESEARCH REPORTS

As far as I have been able to ascertain, the slide rule designed by Professor Swoboda between 1904 and 1909 and the calculation tables originated by Judt and Frueh are the basis of all the presently available calculating and charting devices used today here and abroad. Frueh initiated new research and gave lectures illustrated by projection slides, most of them designed to prove higher accident affinity on the so-called "critical" days. In 1939 he published his first book, *Von der Periodenlehre Zur Biorhythmenlehre* (From Periodicity to the Theory of Biorhythm).* This was followed by *Periodenlehre und Rhythmenpraxis* (The Theory of Periodicity and the Practical Application of Biorhythm).

In his second book, Frueh published numerous medical testimonials and examples, although no statistical documentation was presented. Two additional books were published by Frueh in 1946. One, designed to explain the mathematical evaluation of biorhythm, was entitled *Wie Berechnet und Werted man ein Rhythmogramm?* (How Are Biorhythm Charts Calculated and Evaluated?); the other was *Kraft, Gesundheit und Leistung* (Strength, Health and Performance).* His energetic work can well be considered the new starting point in the acceptance of biorhythm. A number of medical doctors in Switzerland and Germany reported favorably on the use of biorhythm mathematics in cases of selective surgery. The safety engineers of several transportation systems also started to employ the science in accident analysis and accident prevention.

With the growing interest in this type of accident research, Hans Schwing, a student at the Swiss Federal Institute of Technology in Zurich, Switzerland, in 1939 prepared a study relating biorhythm calculations to accident and death statistics. His research report, in the form of a 78-page treatise, is probably one of the most precisely recorded analyses of the subject. This dissertation received high praise from Dr. W. V. Gonzenbach, who at that time

*17*

was director of the Hygienic-Bacteriological Institute at Zurich University, and won for Schwing the title of Doctor of Natural Science.

Schwing's research was based on 700 accident cases, about which data was obtained from Swiss insurance companies and from the workmen's compensation board. In addition, Schwing had collected statistics on 300 deaths from the civil records of the city of Zurich. His analysis was made by employing mathematical formulas for the 23-day, 28-day, and 33-day rhythms of life; it was designed to find out whether man's life actually does flow in a rhythmical pattern. He also wanted to learn whether such a pattern could be traced and possibly used for precalculating any affinity to human error.

His accident analysis was based on the ratio between critical and normal days in a full biorhythmic span, a period of 58 years and 66 or 67 days, depending on the number of interim leap year days.[3]

Schwing also calculated that a span of 21,252 days would mathematically include 4,327 days during which one of the three rhythms would be at a critical point. Such a critical day appears to develop when a rhythm starts a new cycle or changes from the "high" or discharge phase into the "low" or recuperative phase. This second type of critical point is sometimes called the half-periodic day.

In other words, during the span of a biorhythmic life (58 years and 67 or 68 days), man experiences 16,925 days of mixed rhythms and 4,327 days on which a switch or changeover takes place. It is these switch days that are considered potentially critical because then man is believed to show a higher degree of the instability leading to accident, human error, and death affinity. Expressed in percentages, this theoretical ratio is 79.6 percent mixed-rhythm days and 20.4 percent critical days.

In my own research, I have found that the 33-day intellectual rhythm has a minor, or at least only a contributory, influence on human error, accident, or death. Another factor to be considered is

---

[3] A full biorhythmic span is the result of multiplying 23 x 28 x 33 days, a total of 21,252 days. This span of days is the only other point in man's life besides the day of birth when all three rhythms start a new cycle again on the same day.

that the 33-day rhythm has a span almost 1½ times the length of the 23-day physical rhythm, and therefore the 33-day critical days do not occur as often as critical days in the other two rhythms.

Schwing's dissertation showed that of the 700 accidents analyzed, 322 fell on a single critical day, 74 others on a double critical day, and 5 on a triple critical day. The balance (299 accidents) occurred on mixed-rhythm days or what might be called normal days. Thus, a total of 401 accidents (almost 60 percent) out of 700 did occur on critical days, which represent only about 20 percent of the days in man's life, whereas the balance of 299 accidents (about 40 percent) fell on the 80 percent portion of mixed-rhythm days.

This analysis of accidents by means of biorhythm mathematics seems to lend strong support to the theory that man experiences days during which his reflexes and coordination are impaired to the degree of creating a considerably higher disposition toward accident or human error. In an appendix to his statistical report, Schwing pointed out that the accidents were of all types and the cases chosen at random. If purely self-caused accidents had been selected, the percentage would probably have been higher.

For his investigation of a possible relationship between death and biorhythmic disposition, Schwing considered only the 23-day physical and the 28-day sensitivity rhythms. These are the two rhythms that I have found in my own research to be the most telling ones. The 23-day and 28-day rhythms start a simultaneous new upswing every 644 days, or after about one year and nine months. This mathematical span (23 times 28, or 644 days) is called the biorhythmic year; its importance will be explained in later chapters. Schwing apparently did not include the 33-day intellectual rhythm because it would hardly be expected to influence death, except in relatively rare cases of suicide. In this part of his research, he again defined two life patterns, one relating to mixed-rhythm days, respectively the 84.78 percent (based on the two cycles) portion of the so-called normal days in man's life, and the balance of 15.22 percent, representing the potentially critical days.

The mathematical calculations disclosed that of this total of 300 deaths, 197 fell on critical days and the remaining 103 occurred on mixed-rhythm days. The statistics again yielded a surprisingly higher death ratio on biorhythmic critical days. Actually, 65 percent of the deaths fell on the 15 percent portion of the span representing critical days, and only 35 percent coincided with the 85 percent balance of mixed-rhythm days.

Further research in the field of biorhythm mathematics, based on the discoveries by Swoboda and Fliess and applied to accident statistics, is mentioned in numerous articles and reports published in Germany and Switzerland. However, since most of the original documentation was published in what is now East Germany, access to this material is almost impossible to achieve.

In 1962, I secured a copy of an analysis prepared at Humboldt University in Berlin by Reinhold Bochow, under the direction of Dr. J. Sennewald. It was published in the *Wissenschaftliche Zeitschrift der Humboldt Universitaet,* zu Berlin, Jahrgang IV, 1954, Nr. 6. In this investigation of accidents involving workers using agricultural machinery, Bochow used the same mathematical setup of 23-day, 28-day, and 33-day rhythms, and studied 497 accidents. He found that 24.75 percent fell on triple critical days of the workers involved. The triple critical combination occurs, on the average, only about once a year; it is a day when all three cycles cross the zero line simultaneously. This is clearly illustrated in Fig. 6.

Bochow's study claims that another 46.5 percent of the accidents he investigated coincided with a double critical day, such as is shown at A in Fig. 7, and 26.6 percent occurred on a single critical day, such as is shown at B. Only 2.2 percent of the accidents occurred on mixed-rhythm days, a rather startling figure.

In Bochow's treatise, considerable space was devoted to reflecting on the reason for the high accident affinity of workers using agricultural machinery. Bochow carefully considered the biological development of man, and also various factors connected with the causes of these accidents, especially those brought about by psychophysical tendencies. Man, he claimed, is uninhibited and lighthearted in youth; however, youth is quicker in reaction and reflexes. Only later, after gaining experience, does man become more cautious and more considerate of circumstances. But with age he be-

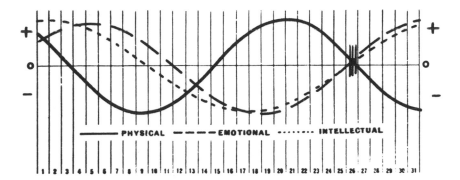

*Fig. 6:* This biorhythm chart shows the triple critical day that the well-known actress and TV star Arlene Francis experienced on May 26, 1963. According to press reports, she lost control of her car, crashed through a dividing barrier, and collided head-on with another vehicle. Calculated on the basis of her reported birth date of October 20, 1912, her physical rhythm on May 26, 1963, was at the switch-point from high to low, and her sensitivity and intellectual rhythms were both at the starting point of a new cycle.

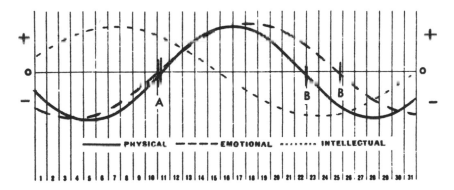

*Fig. 7:* Critical days are the days when a cycle switches from low into high, or from the high period into the low, crossing the zero line. This chart shows a double critical on the 11th of the month, and a critical in the 23-day physical on the 23rd and in the 28-day sensitivity rhythm on the 25th.

*21*

comes slower and less agile too. Improved safety devices and precautionary procedures are, unfortunately, not always successful in preventing accidents because not all workers accept them or take advantage of them to the same degree.

Generally, Bochow claimed, it is not the slow or the lazy worker who is accident-prone; it is the eager and fast worker who gets hurt. As examples he cited a milker who carries a pail of milk and drops it going down a stairway as he trips and falls, or a worker who cuts himself doing a job he has performed thousands of times before without incident. In such accident cases, Bochow explained, where neither the lack of experience nor the newness of the task is the cause of man's disposition, he reacts in relation to what he has set himself out to do. However, man's everyday actions are to a high degree automatic. A person does not, for example, pay attention to every minute detail when he goes down a flight of stairs, consciously thinking of how he takes each step to get out of the building. What follows his original thought of leaving the building is hardly a conscious, concentrated effort for negotiating the steps. If this were not the case, man could not cope with the complexities of everyday life—his consciousness would otherwise be splintered into a multitude of focuses by countless tasks, which could never be completed. Therefore, everyday actions become automatic to a high degree, and this practical, energy-saving automatization results in man's subconscious acceptance of his existence. When, however, subconscious motives are disturbed by rhythmical influences, man becomes prone to err, and is likely to suffer what are called human-error accidents.

Bochow described the numerous tests made with people of both quick and slow reactions, as well as with experienced and inexperienced workers performing both monotonous and tedious work. His final conclusion was that out of 100 accidents, 62 could have been avoided or prevented by personal caution and by having regard for psychophysiological changes in biorhythms.

In September, 1956, a report was released by the Department of Sanitation of the city of Hannover, Germany. It was prepared by the chief engineer, O. Tope, and entitled *Sonderdruck, Staedte-hygiene, Biorhythmische Einfluesse und ihre Auswirkung in Fuhrparkbetrieben* (Special Edition, City Hygiene, The Biorhythmic Powers and Their Effect in the Operation of Trucking Fleets). In this report, accidents suffered by shop workers, street cleaners, and truck drivers were investigated and charted on the basis of the established biorhythm mathematics.

Tope concluded, after analyzing the accidents suffered by street cleaners and shop workers, that 83 percent were related to biorhythmic critical days. He added an interesting observation: in many cases, biorhythmic charting of the drivers involved in a collision clearly indicated which one was at fault.

Although research projects in biorhythm have attracted prime attention in countries outside the United States, some important studies are now being conducted in this country. R. K. Anderson Associates, Inc., a safety consultant firm, has carried out an extensive program of applying biorhythm mathematics to the field of safety. With the kind permission of Mr. R. K. Anderson,[4] the former president of this firm, now retired, I quote from a letter he wrote to me:

Those of us who are in the field of accident prevention are constantly looking for the cause of an accident, and despite intense investigation we may find no other cause than the carelessness of the workman, who in most cases is . . . as thoroughly confused as to why the accident happened.

The first group of accidents studied with Biorhythm produced such fantastic facts that we continued the study for a period of two years with the following results:

1. There was a definite change in the individual during the so-called "critical" days.

2. The study of the accidents showed that the individual

---

4 Russell K. Anderson, Consultant certified by the American Board of Industrial Hygiene for the Comprehensive Practice of Industrial Hygiene.

himself was unaware of this fact and could not understand why the accident occurred.

3. Critical days could be identified as to physical capabilities, mental capacity, as well as the mood of the individual.

Our investigation has covered slightly over three hundred accidents in four industries in which we had available the birth dates of the individuals involved. These plants were a metal working plant, a textile plant, a knitting mill, and a chemical plant.

The investigation was not on a hit-and-miss basis but on a complete analysis of all accidents occurring within the plants over a period of three years in each factory.

The accidents studied were all covered by the Workmen's Compensation Act so that we had detailed and reliable descriptions of each case. All the accidents were analyzed to show the actions of the individual participants. No accidents were included which might have resulted from an extraneous cause.

In our study of over three hundred accidents, we were surprised to find that almost 70 percent of the accidents had occurred on a critical day for the individual involved.

One man who had several accidents presented a puzzle at first because our calculations of the Biorhythm charts were one day off the critical for each accident. You may recall that I telephoned you about this case and you suggested that we check the man's birthplace, which we did. We found that he was born in the Far East under a different date zone and adjusting to this, the Biorhythm charts we had prepared for this man fell into the proper place. This experience contributed considerably to our conviction that Biorhythm calculations are most revealing.

In hazardous work or operations such as one might find in the chemical industry, we feel that there is value to the use of Biorhythm charting where men are in control of dangerous operations.

One accident that points this out was that of a power-press operator who had operated a press for many years without injury; he reached behind the guard of the machine and tripped the press, with the resulting loss of several fingers. Biorhythm analysis showed that at the time of this accident this man was critical in both the mood (28-day) and intelligence (33-day) cycles, and he himself could not explain his actions.

Another accident that has intrigued us was the case of the man lifting a heavy case. He had been told that cases the size he lifted were two-man jobs, but he had decided he could handle it himself, with the result that he sustained a serious back injury. This man was found to be high on all phases Biorhythmically. After talking with the man, we found that he had felt so good that he thought the case could be handled without any help. We did not include this accident as one of those in the 70 percent that we found in critical days.

We are now trying to set up programs with our clients, using the plant supervisors and foremen as key individuals for Biorhythm checks.

In the February, 1973, edition of the *American Society of Safety Engineers Journal,* four and one-half pages were devoted to a report by Mr. R. K. Anderson, from which I quote:

Biorhythm in your hands becomes a wonderful tool to work with. I cannot say that if you have 5000 or even 500 employees in your plant that you should prepare charts for them. We use biorhythm in all places where there is a possibility of a far-reaching and serious accident. The airlines, private pilots, railroad engineers, motormen, truck drivers and salesmen driving cars all day are ideal subjects for biorhythm studies. We have analyzed more than 1000 accidents during the past two years, and the amazing thing is that we have come out with more than 90 percent of the accidents occurring on the critical days.

As a result of my lectures, a number of other pilot projects were put into operation. The titanium division of N. L. Industries tested biorhythm theory in their plant as a device for the prevention of accidents. Reviewing the pilot project after a year and a half, the

Executive Safety Committee of this division reported significant success, and concluded that biorhythm was a practical and effective means of preventing injuries.

Introduced in July, 1965, in the rigging department during a period when the overall injury rate in that division was rising, biorhythm helped the riggers cut their injury rate 18 percent in the second half of 1965 and 42 percent during 1966. The millwright shop, where the accident rate was also showing a steady increase, employed biorhythm during 1966 and reduced injuries 4 percent for that year.

The technique of the pilot project was as follows: biorhythm curves were plotted for each member of the rigging and millwright shops. These data were given to the foremen, who were thus aware of the "critical" days for each individual. The foremen emphasized safety procedures and gave extra supervision to these individuals on their "critical" days. They also bore in mind biorhythmic dispositions when making job assignments, and assigned men in their "critical" days to less hazardous tasks. The pilot project included a control group, the pipe shop, who received just as much attention of a safety-oriented nature as the individuals in the two other divisions, but did not receive guidance based on the principles of biorhythm. During the same period injuries in the pipe shop showed a sharp rise of 28 percent.

## MATHEMATICAL REGULARITY OF BIORHYTHM

*The Flywheel That Keeps Our Clocks on Time: the Rotating Earth*

It is perhaps difficult to accept the regularity and the mathematical accuracy of biorhythm throughout the full span of man's life. However, the studies that resulted in the biorhythm concept suggest that, despite the ups and downs of an individual's life and despite the marked variations between one person's life and another's, the 23-day, 28-day, and 33-day rhythms do continue throughout life with mathematical precision. This must be the case, of course, if we are to predict with confidence what the relative significance of any given rhythm is to be on a specific day, even seventy-five or eighty-five years after birth.

A moment's reflection, on the other hand, will raise troublesome doubts regarding the extraordinary timekeeping accuracy required to maintain these rhythms unvaryingly and completely dependably. Consider the phenomenal accuracy required of a clock that seems to be wound up and "set"—so to speak—at birth, and is never touched thereafter for regulation or adjustment. If such a clock is fast or slow by only one minute per day, this error will grow into a full day in four years, and into five days after twenty years! Can one realistically believe that *every* human being on earth is equipped with not one, but no less than three clocks (a 23-day, a 28-day, and a 33-day clock), each of which keeps such perfect time that even after seventy-five or eighty-five years there is no detectable error?

The most nearly perfect clocks devised by the most advanced techniques of modern science require periodic checking against some super-accurate standard such as the rotation of the earth or, more recently, the vibrations of excited atoms (used for so-called atomic clocks). It is simply too much to believe of a fluctuating, complex, living organism, subject to all the ups and downs of life, that it should rival in precision the most refined mechanism kept under rigidly constant conditions in special laboratories.

The solution to this puzzle seems to be both simple and ingenious. We might say that Nature has devised a way of doing two useful, but somewhat contradictory, things at the same time. First, each infant at birth automatically sets his clock to zero and times his rhythms from that day onward throughout the rest of his life. In this sense the infants born on the same day, within a few hours of each other, form a human subspecies with their own "standard time." Second, all human beings, whatever their individual starting points may be, unconsciously keep their individual clocks from running fast or slow by daily reference to the 24-hour cycle of light and darkness, activity and quiet, which results from the rotation of the earth on its axis. *Thus, although each individual has his own "standard time," all individuals have equally accurate clocks.*

Experimental biology has shown how remarkably widespread throughout nature is this solution to the problem of keeping inner rhythms cycling accurately and in relation to the outside world. As early as the first decade of this century, relevant experiments were reported by the German botanist and naturalist Wilhelm Pfeffer (1845–1920). Pfeffer became interested in the fact that bean seedlings exhibited a rhythmical daily elevation of their leaves *at a specific time* in the morning and a drooping of their leaves *at a specific time* every evening. This phenomenon, called the sleep rhythm of plants, has been extensively studied since.

Suspecting that the daily precise rising and setting of the sun was the influence creating these rhythms in plants, Pfeffer planted some seedlings under constant artificial light and discovered that in such static illumination and unchanging environment they displayed no rhythmical movements. However, when seedlings were sprouted in darkness and given *a single brief exposure to light,* they at once began to exhibit the normal day and night rhythm. This rhythm persisted even after the plants had been returned to darkness. Pfeffer also reported that the time of the day when this single exposure occurred remained the permanent start of leaf movement each subsequent day throughout the life of the plant.

Pfeffer published numerous reports about his research between 1897 and 1915. Some of the findings may be found in *Pflanzenphysiologie,** and in his review *Schlafbewegung der Blattorgane.**

Although it is hazardous to draw parallels between plants and animals and humans, it is nevertheless interesting to note that this observation supports the postulated setting of the rhythmic clocks in human infants by the intense stimulation of all the senses and the initiation of functioning in the new organs during the birth process.

The synchronization of the inner clock in the bean seedlings with the 24-hour rotation of the earth has also been extensively studied. That it is not passively dependent on the duration of light— even in a plant, which is dependent on light for energy to supply all its vital needs—is evident from the remarks of an outstanding modern student of plant rhythms, Fritz W. Went, in *Ecological Implication of the Autonomous 24-Hour Rhythm in Plants:**

. . . the mechanism causing these leaf movements has an autonomous 24-hour rhythm. In nature, this rhythm is usually synchronized with the daily light and dark cycles, but during the long summer days, we usually find that the sleep position of a number of these leaves is already assumed in the early evening hours before darkness has set in, because of the autonomous component of the rhythm.

In animals, the situation appears to be similar. Many bodily functions have been shown to exhibit a 24-hour rhythm under natural conditions. When an animal is subjected to artificial conditions in the laboratory to prevent it from synchronizing its internal rhythmic clocks with the rotation of the earth, these clocks no longer keep the exact 24-hour time, but drift to some other spontaneous, "free-running" value, frequently closer to about 23 hours. But if the animal manages to obtain a few clues to the 24-hour period, it will unconsciously synchronize the spontaneous autonomous rhythms so that they again become 24 hours in length.

In *Physiologic 24-Hour Periodicity,* * Dr. Franz Halberg, an outstanding investigator of biological rhythms, who is associated with the University of Minnesota School of Medicine, has demonstrated this resynchronization in his studies of the 24-hour cycle of fluctuations in the body temperature of mice. If mice are experimentally blinded and the 24-hour cycle of light and darkness is removed as a governor or synchronizer, the rhythm of body temperature gradually shifts toward a 23-hour free-running cycle for two to three months. Starting in the third month, however, the rhythm begins to shift back to its normal 24-hour value, and by five months there is no discernible difference in the timing from normal! The explanation appears to be that in the absence of the dominant sense of eyesight, the other senses—hearing, feeling (vibrations), smell, etc.— take over the function of synchronizing the internally generated rhythm of temperature fluctuations with the 24-hour cycle based on the rotation of the earth.

Studies of dreams, according to Dr. William C. Dements, a neurophysiologist at Stanford University School of Medicine, suggest that the nervous system is the font of dreams. To those curious about the regularity of biorhythm, it is interesting to learn from these dream studies that after subjects were deprived of dreams during successive nights, their mental reactions became highly suspicious, at times resembling psychotic derangement. However, on nights when the subjects were again allowed to dream, the *length of the dream time was increased proportionally* to the duration of dream deprivation. In these studies we again find evidence of subtle governors taking over the work of speeding up a rhythm after it was forcefully put out of phase.

Although most modern experimenters have concentrated on short-term rhythms, such as 24-hour cycles, the same basic principles would seem to apply to longer-term rhythms, such as those emphasized by biorhythm mathematics. Indeed, it is the author's hope that calling attention to the pioneering work upon which biorhythm mathematics is based will stimulate further experimental work in this important field, which promises so much for human health, happiness, and understanding.

## WHAT IS BIORHYTHM?

Swoboda, Fliess, Schlieper, and others who pursued the basic studies of long-term rhythmic cycles and discovered the 23-day and the 28-day rhythms ascribed these fluctuations to charges and discharges in the cell system. Scientists of today use the term "biological clocks" for a variety of cyclical or rhythmical changes in the human body. It has become a recognized fact of science that all life, down to the single cell, is regulated by a rhythmical pulsation. It would appear presumptuous to assume that these natural "beats" are not of a highly organized nature.

The question of whether such basically regulated long-term rhythms can be observed and even predetermined over periods of weeks, months, and years is most interesting. If they can—and the studies and research presented in this book would lend considerable credence to this idea—the practical benefits of biorhythm for every individual in all walks of life could be invaluable.

My personal interest in the observation of rhythmic cycles in life goes back to 1946, when a friend brought me one of Frueh's calculators from Switzerland and explained the theory of the mathematical regularity to me. Skeptical at first, I started to calculate the biorhythmic disposition of athletes prior to sports events or tournaments. To my surprise, the biorhythm charts disclosed an amazing accuracy; however, I wanted more definite proof of the regularity of these rhythms, and I began charting accidents and deaths whenever I was able to obtain reliable birth, accident, and death information. Again my research demonstrated the regularity of the rhythms to a high degree.

Unfortunately, the time I could devote to this study was limited, and I found the Biocalculator too cumbersome and slow in preparing large numbers of charts for research. For this reason, I equipped myself with a set of basic calculation tables similar to those originally developed by Judt and Frueh. These tables have been brought up to date in this book; they will enable anyone who can add or subtract to calculate his or her biorhythmic position in advance for any month up until December, 2008. The tables have also been extended backward to 1982 so that the reader who has kept a diary can check back on events in his life to find confirmation of the accuracy of biorhythm mathematics and of the regularity of his own cycles. The ease of making such charts should induce people interested in their own safety and in the study of human behavior to chart their good and bad days. I have also prepared an annual master calculation book containing the final biorhythm figures for any birth date in relation to the current year. This aggregate of over 40,000 figures is designed for use by researchers in safety and medicine; it offers the fastest and easiest method of preparing large numbers of charts.

## THE DEVELOPMENT OF BIORHYTHMIC CHARTING METHODS

From my studies of the available books by Swoboda, Fliess, and Schlieper, the three best-known proponents of biorhythm, I could not determine how these men had calculated the variations of the two basic rhythms. The examples in their books—and there are thousands—are all expressed in mathematical formulas and in relation to calendar data. Swoboda, who pursued his studies independently in Vienna, apparently had his slide rules made specifically to find the critical days and he did not publicize the device. Perhaps

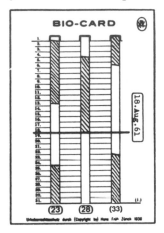

*Fig 8:* The vertical type of biorhythm chart produced by Hans Frueh, Zurich, to show the three biorhythms in relation to the days of a month. The horizontal line indicates a critical day in the 28-day sensitivity cycle, with a complete low in the 23-day physical cycle.

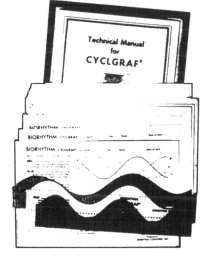

*Fig. 9:* The CYCLGRAF is a charting kit with calculation tables, chart blanks, and calibrated cycle rulers.

32

this was another one of the stumbling blocks that prevented broader acceptance of the theory. From some reports, one gets the impression that ordinary graph paper was used to plot the rhythms, with their interweaving patterns and critical points.

With the advent of additional studies and the development of the calculation tables and calculators, Frueh in Switzerland designed a vertical type of chart that corresponded with the band arrangement he had incorporated in the calculator. These card-type vertical charts are still in use abroad. The "plus" portion or first half of each rhythm is drawn in color, red for the 23-day physical (masculine) rhythm, blue for the 28-day sensitivity (feminine) rhythm, and green for the 33-day intellectual rhythm. The second half or "minus" portion is left blank against the respective dates so that the beginning as well as the halfway mark of each rhythm can be seen readily in order to determine the critical biorhythmic days.

To facilitate the making of biorhythm charts, a sine-curve type was developed during the 1950's. This type, which is used in all the examples shown in this book, seems to be more readily understood and easier to draw. It also clearly shows the relative changes of the three rhythms day by day. The upper half of the chart represents the plus periods, and the lower half the minus or recuperative periods. Cycle rulers are designed so that the days of the calculated rhythms can be positioned over the first day of the month, and all the following days and rhythm positions will then fall into line, as shown in Fig. 10, where the ruler for the 23-day physical rhythm is superimposed, with the 14th day of this rhythm on the first of the month.

BIORHYTHM
CYCLGRAF®
U.S. Patent Pending

BIO-CALENDAR, INC.

RED curve represents the 23 day cycle of physical strength, endurance, energy, resistance, confidence.

*Fig. 10:* The 23-day cycle ruler has been placed over a biorhythm chart, with the 14th day of the cycle starting the month.

*33*

Although biorhythm charts of the sine-curve type show the ups and downs more dramatically, they should not be interpreted as indicating the degree or amplitude of the high or low points in a rhythm. Here again, one must carefully consider health, character, age, and other factors affecting a person. It is suggested that for older and generally calmer people the peaks and the valleys are not as extreme as they appear to be in the case of younger and more temperamental individuals. However, statistics seem to indicate that the propensity for accident or human error on the critical day is equally pronounced in youth and in old age. No standard pattern should therefore be assumed, and each individual must be guided by self-observation.

On the other hand, some of the most recent research into accident statistics appears to indicate that if, for instance, a critical day exists in the 28-day (sensitivity) rhythm, in combination with a top high in the 23-day (physical) rhythm, the degree of accident affinity is increased. Possibly a dominating exuberance in the physical disposition, at a moment when mental coordination is impaired by a critical day, creates a pattern of "matter over mind."

In later pages of this book, numerous examples are given showing biorhythm applied to sports, accidents, deaths, and various other happenings. These examples should be considered typical rather than exceptional. They are included merely to illustrate the accuracy of the rhythms in man and to demonstrate that this mathematical regularity can be used to review events of the past, as well as to indicate human disposition for days, weeks, even years in advance. In some cases, both the original mathematical method of calculation and the use of the calculation tables are shown, in proof of the fact that biorhythm mathematics leaves no room for variation or guesswork.

## THE SKEPTICS

Although skepticism can at times save a person from making mistakes or coming to impulsive decisions, a completely closed mind can be destructive to progress. The science of biorhythm has

# BIORHYTHM CYCLGRAF®

for Month _____ Year _____ Name _____ Date of birth _____

How to interpret your biorhythmic cycles.

**RED** curve represents the 23 day cycle of physical strength, endurance, energy, resistance, confidence.

**BLUE** curve shows the 28 day cycle governing sensibility, nerves, feelings, intuition, cheerfulness, moodiness, creative ability.

**GREEN** curve is for the 33 day cycle of intelligence, memory, mental alertness, logic, reasoning power, reaction, ambition.

physical ——————   sensitivity – – – –   intellect - - - - -

1 2 3 4 5 6 7 8 9 10 11 12 13 14 15 16 17 18 19 20 21 22 23 24 25 26 27 28 29 30 31

**+**  The period above the horizontal a-line shows the days of full vitality and efficiency, and when we are at our best and can endure the most.

**–**  The period below the horizontal a-line shows the days of reduced efficiency, when our system recuperates and when we are not as sharp and keen, and tire more easily.

During mixed-curve periods i.e., when the RED curve is high and the BLUE or the GREEN curve is down, we can do great things physically but must watch our sensibility or mental alertness. The reverse position of these cycles would indicate soundness in our sensibility or mental alertness, but physically we become tired more easily.

**o**  Critical days in biorhythm are those when the RED or the BLUE curve passes through the horizontal a-line; either on the way up or down. On such a day our substance or cells seem to be in a state of "flux" or at a switch-point during which, according to statistics we are from 7 to 8 times more accident prone.

**o + o**  If a "critical day" curve coincides with a complete low, or with a critical day of another cycle, our biorhythmic condition should warn us to be extra cautious.

## BIO-CALENDAR, INC.
P.O. BOX 66509 ST. PETERSBURG BEACH, FL 33736

**COPYRIGHT 1984**

been suffering from the influences of skeptics and, on the other hand, from the exaggerated claims of promoters who offered it as a panacea. Perhaps Fliess's introduction to the fifth edition of his book, *Vom Leben und Vom Tod* (Of Life and of Death) is most appropriate:

The point I wish to make clear is the assumption that all life follows an internal regulated pattern, a mechanism which is alike in man, in animal and in plant; a mechanism which regulates the hour of birth to the same accuracy as the hour of death. If you hear of the passing of an hour, you think of the mechanism of the clock. However, there is a great difference between the ticking off of time by a clock, compared to the flow of life. The clock has a uniform momentum, each hour is exactly like the next. Events in life, however, follow regular paths. Distances of time vary between birth in the same family. The length of pregnancy differs with the same mother.

In nature, blossoms open at different times, and even the migration of birds falls on different days over a period of years. It is these variations which cause some to be skeptical about the regularity of the basic rhythms in man. One seems to be more inclined to pay close attention to generalities, such as the weather, or the will of God. Perhaps, just considering generalities is not enough. The first blossoms of spring often come too early, even some of the swallows may come ahead of schedule, and in the fall an icy blast often fails to drive our migrating birds southward—as long as their internal timers which urge them to fly south have not yet executed their great power.

Scientists have observed these irregularities, but many of them have not gone beyond this question mark. My readers, let me ask you: does an irregularity in one field presuppose that the laws of nature are wrong? Isn't it a fact that gravity, the rotation of the earth around the sun, are irregular? And did not Galileo, Kepler, Newton, and others explain the variations in these laws? Therefore, irregularities alone cannot eliminate laws.

# 3

# BIORHYTHM AND HOW IT WORKS

## THE 23-DAY PHYSICAL RHYTHM

The 23-day rhythm was believed by Fliess to originate in the muscular cells or fibers. Its fluctuations affect man's physical strength, endurance, energy, resistance, and physical confidence. The first half of the cycle—11½ days in duration—is the ascending or discharge period; these are the days when a person feels vigorous and when his vitality and endurance are at their best, when physical work seems easier. Athletes generally perform best during this plus period. Doctors abroad who consider biorhythm charting as part of any diagnosis select the period between the second and ninth days of the cycle as the most favorable for selective surgery.

The second half of the 23-day rhythm is known as the recharging period. During these 11½ days a person is inclined to tire more easily; for example, athletes (depending upon the position of their other rhythms) often find themselves in a slump, having less reserve power, energy, or endurance. Medical men consider the recharging periods as conducive to recuperation because, by nature, a patient is more likely to accept this period as restful. This generalization is, of course, only relative. All other things being equal, a trained athlete can succeed even during a recuperative period if he has not overtrained prior to the contest.

It is also necessary to consider outside influences that may affect certain days; although a person can learn to recognize his own behavior pattern in advance, he cannot control the world around him or divine the effect outside events will have. This second portion of the 23-day physical rhythm—the 11½ days of relatively reduced strength and endurance—is by no means all "bad" days; in fact, this period can be advantageous for the athlete who wishes to train intelligently. The practicing of routine exercises will help him to get his subconscious reaction and timing "in the groove." Knowledge of his biorhythm disposition will make him cautious about over-training, which is frequently blamed when a potential success is apparently ruined by lack of reserve power. Most of us, and particularly athletes, have experienced this situation. Perhaps the battery and generator of a car offer a practical comparison. When the battery is fully charged, the current sparks the ignition to full power; after the battery has run down, the generator switches in, bringing the charge to full power again.

The two important points in this rhythm are the first day, when a new cycle begins, and the halfway mark (11½ days), when one's energy switches into the recharge or minus period. These days are the critical or flux days. The full meaning of a critical day will be explained in a later chapter.

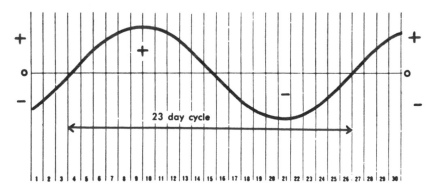

*Fig. 11:* This chart shows the 23-day physical rhythm starting a new cycle on the 4th of the month and ending it on the 26th. The first 11½ days are the plus or high period; the second 11½ days are the days of recharge or recuperation.

38

# THE 28-DAY SENSITIVITY RHYTHM

The 28-day rhythm governs the nervous system. It was ascribed by Fliess to the influence on the cells of man's feminine inheritance. This sensitivity rhythm too is divided into half-periods. The first 14 days represent the plus or discharge period during which a person is more inclined to optimism and cheerfulness. This period favorably influences creative enterprise, feelings, love, cooperation, and all coordination that is connected with the nervous system. The second half, from the 15th to the 28th day, represents the recuperative or recharge period during which a person is more inclined to become irritable and negative. Excitable people will find their sensitivity extremes more noticeable than calmer people who are known for their even disposition. Excitable people should find the observation of this rhythm in their emotional feelings particularly meaningful.

The 28-day sensitivity rhythm registers its critical days during the first day of a new cycle and again during the 15th day, when the phase switches into the recuperative period of 14 days. The critical days should be watched, especially by drivers and by anyone else who depends on his ability to react quickly and with sound judgment. The percentage of self-caused accidents occurring on critical sensitivity days provides additional powerful evidence of the regular

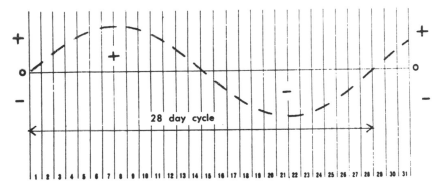

*Fig. 12:* The 28-day sensitivity cycle is divided into a 14-day period of plus and a 14-day period of minus or recuperative days.

influence of these rhythms. The affinity for error and accident is greater yet, as was made clear by the researches of Schwing, Bochow, Tope, and Anderson, when such a critical day coincides with a critical day in the physical rhythm. Fortunately, such double critical combinations occur, on the average, less than six times a year, and even if they are present, a person is not necessarily powerless to avoid accident or human error.

Readers who are mathematically inclined will appreciate the fact that since the 28-day rhythm is composed of four seven-day weeks, the weekday that one was born on will always repeat on the first and on the fifteenth day of this rhythm. Therefore, someone born on a Wednesday, for example, can plan that every second Wednesday will represent a day of higher affinity for accidents, or human error. He can benefit from this knowledge by taking additional precautions on these alternate Wednesdays. The invariability of this cycle also permits a person who does not know the day of the week he was born on to find this important day by calculating his 28-day biorhythm.

As far as can be ascertained from the documentation of the pioneers Fliess and Swoboda, the discovery of regulated rhythms in life was based on an empirical evaluation. More recent scientific and medical discoveries, however, seem to provide actual physical proof of the existence of rhythmical pulsations in life. During the meeting of the National Academy of Sciences in Washington in April, 1962, Professor Paul A. Weiss of the Rockefeller Institute demonstrated with motion pictures how the nerve fiber flows like a "river with a rhythmical beat" from its mainspring in the nervous system. Dr. Weiss explained that the nerve fiber, like any cell, continually consumes and replenishes its substance and is continually flowing. The conventional concept had been that the nerve structure was a rigid system which, once in a position, served only to carry messages as telephone lines do.

That same month, the *New York State Journal of Medicine* reported on a study of "The Direct Current Control System: A Link Between Environment and Organism" by Robert O. Becker, M.D., Charles H. Bachman, Ph.D., and Howard Friedman, Ph.D., from the State University of New York Upstate Medical Center, the Veterans Administration Hospital, and Syracuse University:

> Since the cranial Direct Current potential appeared to be a particularly important parameter in the state of consciousness or level of irritability in the human being, the possibility that it was the controlling mechanism for biologic cyclic behavior was considered. In a very preliminary study the transcranial D.C. potential of two normal subjects and two schizophrenic patients was determined daily for a period of two months. A definite cyclic pattern was evident in all four subjects, with a periodicity of approximately *twenty-eight* days and with all four following similar cycles.

Perhaps a correlation of this recent discovery of a 28-day rhythm in transcranial D.C. potential with the biorhythm mathematics explained in this book would be a very interesting project in man's efforts to find a universal tide of life.

## THE 33-DAY INTELLECTUAL RHYTHM

The 33-day intellectual rhythm apparently originates in the brain cells. Teltscher's associates and also certain doctors ascribed the phenomenon to a secretion of the thyroid gland. The first 16½ days of this rhythm are the days when students were found to be more capable of absorbing new subjects. During the first half of this rhythm one can think more clearly, the memory functions well, and mental response is most spontaneous. This period is considered the best time to absorb new subjects, and for studying and creative thinking. Knowledge of this fact should be helpful to students, writers, scientists, and artists.

The second 16½ days in the 33-day cycle represent the period when the capacity to think is reduced, when students generally find it more difficult to absorb new subjects, and when it would be more expedient to review and to rehearse previously studied subjects. It is the best time to practice, in order to store knowledge in the subconscious mind and memory.

One of the scientists with whom I discussed this 33-day intellectual rhythm explained its effect by comparing a learner-driver with an experienced driver. "A learner-driver," he said, "while listening to the instructor, will transfer the lesson via the brain to his muscular or physical system." Every time he has to shift gears, use the brake, the accelerator, or the steering wheel, the impulse to do so is derived from a conscious thought. After he has become experienced, these impulses or directions from the brain to the muscular or physical system become so mechanical that an experienced driver actually drives with his subconscious mind; his efforts, judgment, in fact his driving-thinking, become automatic functions governed by the 28-day rhythm of the sensitivity cycle or nervous system described in the preceding section. The individual can only hope that his automatic pilots do the right thing at the right time.

The critical days in the 33-day intellectual cycle are, again, the days a person must observe more closely. They are the first and the seventeenth day, representing respectively the start and the halfway mark of the 33-day rhythm. It is wise to know when these days occur, especially if a person has to make an important decision or sign important papers. If at all possible, important decisions should be postponed for better days; if that cannot be done, every effort should be made to think things out clearly in advance.

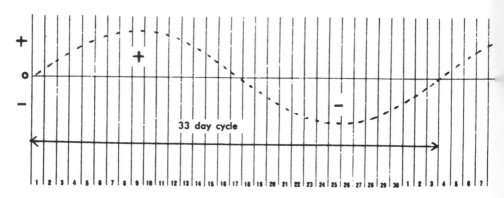

Fig. 13: A complete cycle in the 33-day intellectual rhythm. This rhythm is divided into two 16½-day periods of plus and minus, as shown in the chart.

The word *critical* can be defined as "full of danger or difficulty." This definition best describes the critical position or day in the biorhythm theory. Since the accident analyses shown on earlier pages were prepared, thousands of additional cases have confirmed the higher potential for human error on critical days. These statistics also confirm the basic theory discovered by Swoboda and Fliess that man's life is governed by rhythmical fluctuations that create his ups and downs.

In the explanations already given of each of the three rhythms, the critical days were defined as the first day of a new cycle and the day when a rhythm changes from its high or discharge phase into the recuperating phase. Both these days are considered critical, the second type being sometimes referred to as the half-periodic day.

The critical day phenomenon can be compared with what happens to an electric light bulb. When a light bulb blows out, it usually does so with a flash the moment the switch is turned on. An electrician would explain that this happens because the current, suddenly entering a cold filament, causes it to snap if it has become weak physically. The second most frequent time when light-bulb filaments fail is the moment when the current is turned off.

Critical days may be considered the switch-point days. A person should be more careful during these critical days because his system seems to be in a state of flux and to have a considerable degree of instability. Critical days *in themselves* are not dangerous. Rather, they are days during which the individual's reaction to his environment may bring about a critical situation. Biorhythm does not, and should not be expected to, predict future behavior or accidents, for the way a person acts depends on what is happening *to* him, as well as on the condition he happens to be in physically, emotionally, and intellectually at a particular time.

The great advantage of biorhythmic theory is that the pattern of critical days can easily be predetermined. Since these days represent less than 20 percent of an individual's life it should not be too much trouble to set up safeguards and take precautions on such days. The saying "forewarned is forearmed" seems most appropriate to anyone who has studied biorhythm calculations.

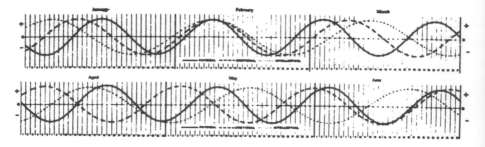

*Fig. 14:* This reduced-scale biorhythm chart covering a period of six months shows how the rhythms change constantly in relation to one another, although they keep their own 23-day, 28-day, and 33-day regularity.

## THE CRITICAL PERIOD, AND THE IMPORTANCE OF THE HOUR OF BIRTH

The critical day or period is estimated to last twenty-four hours. Since no conclusive biological research results are available, we make this estimate empirically, on the basis of accident analysis.

Experience indicates that knowledge of the exact hour of birth can be of some importance. A person born immediately after midnight or during the early morning hours will be almost a day old when another baby, born during the last hour of the *same day,* takes its first breath. Knowing the hour of birth, or at least the approximate time of day, makes it possible to draw the biorhythm chart more accurately. In general, people born during the morning hours will experience their critical period during the day in the chart based on the actual birthday, whereas people born late that same day may find their biorhythm situation in the chart based on the day after birth. Just how these variations can be reflected in the drawing of biorhythm charts is shown in Fig. 15.

In my own research, I have encountered a number of striking examples where the hour of birth at either side of midnight was directly reflected in a critical-day accident. One observer of bio-

*44*

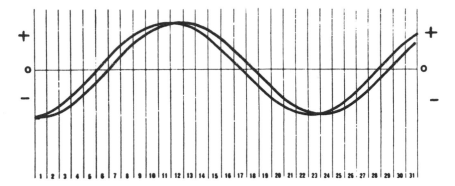

Fig. 15: In this chart, one line was drawn to represent a cycle beginning with a birth during the early hours of a day. The second line shows the slightly different location of a rhythm line for a birth during the late hours of the same day.

rhythm, for example, complained that his calculations were always a day off. He had kept a diary for over twenty years and had gone to the trouble of reviewing and charting many of his experiences. These included a broken leg he had sustained while skating and an automobile accident he had caused by turning into the wrong end of a one-way street. Both accidents had occurred on a Sunday morning—a day *after* the critical day designated by his biorhythm chart. The accidents were so typical of the human-error type, and had occurred at so nearly the identical hour, that it seemed the discrepancy might be found by checking the hour of birth. "Oh, yes," he remarked, "I was born just a few minutes *before* midnight. My mother often said she hurried my arrival all she could because she wanted a Sabbath child, a tradition in her family." Adjusting the cycles almost a day to make allowance for the hour of birth brought all the calculations into line.

For every person who is convinced, and is aware of the changing feelings he experiences, there is somebody else who simply "has to be shown." The science of biorhythm, fortunately, is exact enough so that almost everyone can be shown whether the theory is, in fact, meaningful.

There are those, however, who are disposed to think that

man's life is predestined in every detail and that accidents and errors are quite unavoidable. The late Joe Jacobs is remembered as the boxing promoter who coined the phrase: "He should have stood in bed." This twenty-twenty hindsight is also typically expressed by "I wish I had known!" Biorhythm can go a long way toward fulfilling that wish, simply by providing a great deal more knowledge about a person's own future potential and, hence, enabling him to take definite steps to anticipate the effects of his ups and downs.

**4**

# APPLYING THE THEORY OF BIORHYTHM

## FORESIGHT IS WISDOM

To quote Alexander Hamilton: "Instead of being ruled by accident, we can govern ourselves by reflection and choice." Knowledge is, in fact, considered supreme by most people.

The knowledge of biorhythm allows a person to ascertain his disposition in advance, at any time and for any occasion. This forewarning may save him agony, despair, financial loss, even tragedy; but, in any case, the very least it will do is to tell him more about himself.

Several years ago I met a group of flight commanders from the United States Naval Safety Center at Norfolk, Virginia. We were discussing biorhythm mathematics, and I was given certain data on seventeen recent flight accidents: actually, only the date of birth of the pilot and the *month* each accident had occurred. After calculating these human-error cases, I estimated *the most probable days* on which the accidents might have happened. The estimates, based purely on the critical-day potential in each case, proved correct in twelve out of the seventeen cases, and so were more than 70 percent accurate, a percentage that would seem to eliminate chance. When I suggested, however, that in the future the pilots should be given an opportunity to know the days during which a potential increase in danger might be in store for them, the officer in charge remarked:

*47*

"We tell them to be careful every day." I would recommend that pilots be warned of their critical days whenever they are to undertake difficult maneuvers or face hazardous conditions.

As Lord Beacon noted: "We can only dominate nature by subjecting ourselves to its laws." To those who have followed the research in biorhythm, these rhythms are part of the laws of nature.

## INNER RHYTHMS IN OUTER SPACE

Few events in recent history have excited the imagination as much as the news of launching astronauts into space. While millions of people in the United States and around the world watched their television screens or listened to radio reports, Shepard, Grissom, Glenn, Carpenter, and Schirra risked their lives, trusting the perfect functioning of the many intricate and delicate launching, flight, and re-entry devices. When I calculated the biorhythmic disposition of each astronaut, an even greater element of suspense was added for me! Grissom and Carpenter both were at a point where the affinity for human error was high, and therefore, when the news of Grissom's difficulties and of the subsequent loss of the $5,000,000 capsule with all its precious data came over the air, my anxiety concerning Grissom's safety was heightened. The biorhythm chart reproduced here shows the two critical days that coincided with his launching date, and that may have had a significant effect on his inability to cope with the complexity of his circumstances.

Grissom's poor biorhythmic disposition, as foretold by his chart, would tend to increase the chance of human error under the pressure of such a stress situation; he would tend to be high-strung and, in addition, handicapped by the low in his intellectual rhythm. But it is also necessary to take into consideration the years of hard training these astronauts undergo under simulated flight conditions. The example given earlier of a learning driver and man's built-in automatic pilot exemplifies how the results of constant practice are stored up, so that after a thorough initiation program most functions become largely subconscious actions. With hazardous ventures, however, man must always reckon on unexpected turns of events, such as mechanical failure in any one of the thousands of compo-

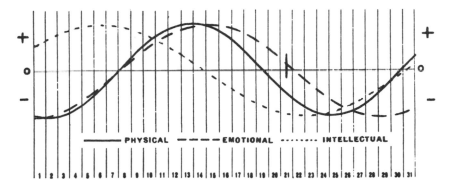

*Fig. 16:* Capt. Virgil I. Grissom, born April 3, 1926, was launched for one orbit on July 21, 1961. On landing, his hatch blew open for unaccountable reasons, causing the capsule to fill with water and sink. Grissom almost drowned. His biorhythmic disposition on July 21, 1961, shows him near the critical point in his sensitivity cycle, with both his physical and intellectual cycles low.

nents that comprise a space vehicle. But human error is still considered the essential factor, and often the least understood.

Lieutenant Colonel John H. Glenn, Jr., who orbited the earth three times on February 20, 1962, had better luck. He missed a critical biorhythmic day in sensitivity by a scant day, and had only his intellectual cycle in high. A preferable biorhythmic condition would have been a launch between February 7 and 15, or after March 7.

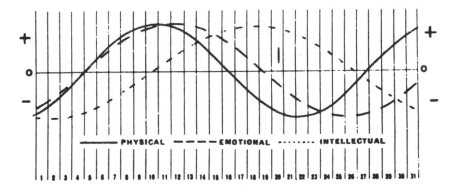

*Fig. 17:* Lt. Col. John H. Glenn, Jr., born on July 18, 1921, made three orbits around the earth on February 20, 1962. His physical and sensitivity rhythms were low and his intellectual rhythm high.

The three-orbit flight of Lieutenant Commander M. Scott Carpenter on May 24, 1962 almost had a tragic ending. The day of his adventurous flight indicated a critical position in the sensitivity rhythm, an intellectual high, and a physical low. As previously noted, the highs and lows do not have as profound an influence on the human-error element as the critical days. This is especially true if two of the rhythms are in opposition to each other—that is, one high and the other low—since there is evidence that an element of adjustment or compensation takes place. In Carpenter's case, it evidently was the critical in his sensitivity rhythm that may have made the difference. According to reports, he erred by using too much fuel, leaving the automatic control system on while also using fuel for the manual operation to stabilize the capsule during orbit. On re-entry, the space ship was not tilted at the correct angle, and for anxious minutes Carpenter was lost to the world. These errors caused him to overshoot the intended landing site by some 250 miles. In a subsequent newspaper interview Carpenter apologized for his "cliff-hanger." Here again, biorhythmic charting clearly shows the human-error potential for Carpenter on May 24, 1962.

In the case of Commander Walter M. Schirra, his favorable biorhythmic position during his six-orbit trip on October 3, 1962 was reflected in his excellent performance during all phases of his flight, the pinpoint landing in the Pacific Ocean, and his action of

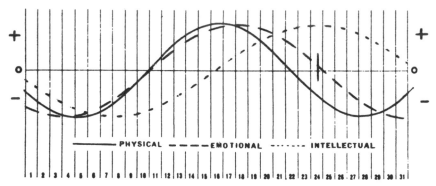

*Fig. 18:* Capt. M. Scott Carpenter, born May 1, 1931, was launched for a three-orbit flight on May 24, 1962. He overshot his landing target by 250 miles. The biorhythm chart shows him near the critical point in his sensitivity cycle, low in his physical cycle, and high only in the intellectual cycle.

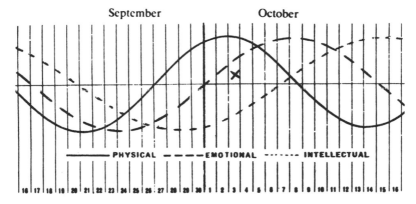

September          October

——————— PHYSICAL  — — — — EMOTIONAL  ········ INTELLECTUAL

*Fig. 19:* Comdr. Walter M. Schirra, Jr., born March 12, 1923, completed six orbits on October 3, 1962, and made a pinpoint landing on target in the Pacific. He was high in both physical and sensitivity cycles, low only in the intellectual cycle.

remaining calmly inside the capsule until he had been hoisted onto the deck of the aircraft carrier.

Perhaps it should be reiterated that the purpose of biorhythm is not necessarily to predict accidents or error; it is designed to ascertain, in advance, the *potential* human disposition on a particular day. Unless external events place the individual in a potentially dangerous situation, critical days will ordinarily pass unnoticed except by the keenest observers.

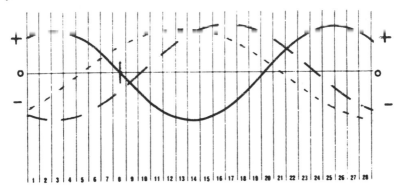

*Fig. 20:* Dr. Edgar D. Mitchell, born September 17, 1930. The Apollo 14 astronaut realized after takeoff from the moon, February 9, 1971, that he had overlooked removing the protective cover from the lens of a camera positioned to photograph the launch back to earth. Could the critical position in his physical rhythm on February 8, 1971, have contributed to this human error?

*51*

# AVIATION AND HUMAN ERROR

The application of biorhythm to the study of aircraft accidents where human failure is suspected has variously been reported as being part of a routine procedure by some of the airlines abroad. However, the officials I was able to reach were reluctant to confirm such studies for fear the public might misunderstand this type of human-error investigation. It was also pointed out that an airline could hardly risk placing reliance on pilots largely on the basis of such an apparently unorthodox procedure.

In continuing my search for aviation accident data, I checked with the Daniel & Florence Guggenheim Aviation Safety Center at Cornell University. The high safety record established by commercial airlines owes a great debt to the Guggenheim Aviation Safety Center and its unbiased fact-finding reports. The center was established, however, primarily to investigate and to appraise the safety features of aircraft instrumentation, and it does not possess the funds that would be needed to initiate a large-scale research study of pilot error in relation to accident statistics. The limited study of accidents involving private pilots for which the Safety Center was able to obtain complete and reliable data produced convincing proof that biorhythm should become part of all such accident research.

The use of biorhythm aids by private aircraft pilots deserves special consideration. Private pilots usually fly smaller planes, which do not have the complex, expensive, and tested safety instrumentation with which commercial airliners are equipped. Furthermore, the safety regulations prescribed by the Federal Aviation Agency are not as rigid for private pilots as they are for commercial airline pilots.

Of the cases charted for the Aviation Safety Center, about 80 percent coincided with a critical day of the pilot; there was one case where both pilot and co-pilot had identical rhythms and critical days, apparently a contributing factor in causing them to crash.

Lyndon Johnson, then Vice-President, answered my request of February 21, 1961, for the birth dates of his two pilots who had crashed during the night of February 19. Captain Harold Teague and Captain Charles Williams were bringing President Johnson's plane in from another airport that night. News reports stated that the pilots experienced delays in starting their flight and that the weather became increasingly bad. As they prepared for a landing on the airfield of the LBJ ranch, a rainstorm cut down visibility. Had they been thirty feet higher, they would have missed the hill against which they crashed. Both men were killed. Teague and Williams were excellent and experienced pilots; however, their biorhythm charts disclosed that both had critical days, which, combined with exhaustion and hazardous flying conditions, apparently culminated in dramatic evidence of human failure.

In March of 1972, Tim Brady, Major, USAF and editor of *TAC Attack,* published by the Department of the Air Force, Head-

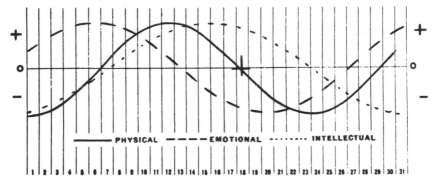

PHYSICAL ————EMOTIONAL ········ INTELLECTUAL

*Fig. 21-A:* Capt. Harold Teague, born December 27, 1920.

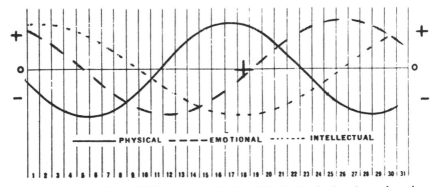

PHYSICAL ————EMOTIONAL ········ INTELLECTUAL

*Fig. 21-B:* Capt. Charles Williams, born July 30, 1922. The biorhythm charts show that both pilots were at a critical day on February 18, when they started their ill-fated flight.

quarters of the Tactical Air Command, Langley Air Force Base, Virginia, included the following report about biorhythm:

The total sample was composed of 59 accidents wherein only the pilots involved were analyzed. Of those 59 accidents, 13 occurred on a critical biorhythmic day for at least one of the pilots involved. In 12 of the 13 accidents the pilot involved was either an IP AC or in a single place airplane. Not as significant, but still worth a mention, is the fact that in 40 (67 percent) of the 59 accidents at least one of the pilots involved had two or more biorhythmic cycles in the minus portion.

The most important fact is that Major Brady made these studies on his own and evidently used the calculation tables, cycle rulers, and chart blanks in a previous edition of this book.

## THE TRAGEDY OF AIRLINE CRASHES

With the introduction of modern jet airliners and the intense enforcement of safety rules by the Federal Aviation Agency and the National Transportation Board, flying has become one of the safest methods of distance transportation. Our giant airliners—and there are over 25,000 commercial aircraft in the air every hour of the day—are equipped with superhuman sophisticated safety devices; however, human frailty is basically the same as it has been in the past. No matter how well trained and experienced, men still make errors. Evidence in recent tragic accidents indicates that the application of the biorhythm theory might have prevented such losses. One should overlook no device that might afford an insight into the biological response of a crew in charge of hundreds of passengers. It is especially urgent to make the biorhythm theory better known because in an alarmingly high percentage of recent airliner crashes "human error" was suspected as the cause. We must overcome resistance to classifying the biorhythm theory as a form of astrology. Biorhythm charts are not calculated to predict the fate of a person or accidents, but to warn of periods requiring especial care. Preknowledge of an error-prone day would not create a subconscious compulsion to commit an error any more than road warning

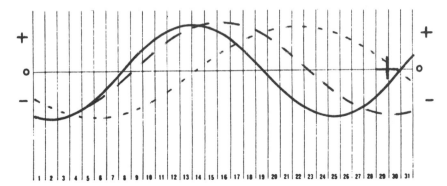

*Fig. 22-A:* Captain Robert A. Loft, born March 17, 1917, pilot of the ill-fated Eastern Airlines new giant Lockheed L-1011 TriStar jet with 176 on board from New York. He had turned over the landing procedures to First Officer Stockstill prior to the crash on December 29, 1972, in the swampy Everglades 18 miles west of Miami Airport. Associated Press reports stated that the loss of 101 lives was caused because the crew was preoccupied trying to find out why the red warning light showed, indicating the nose wheel had failed to lower. Captain Loft's biorhythm chart shows him near critical in the intellectual rhythm with a physical critical only a few hours away.

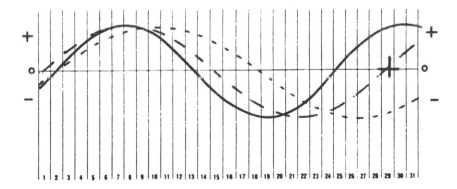

*Fig. 22-B:* First Officer A. J. Stockstill, born June 8, 1933, in charge of landing, evidently was watching the other crew members and did not notice the jet was rapidly losing altitude. Could this human-error tragedy on December 29, 1972, have been avoided if Stockstill had known his biorhythm disposition on that day? The IBM-360 computer programmed biorhythm report I had prepared for Time Pattern Research Institute a few months before, read as follows: "STOP! LOOK! LISTEN! It's one of your off days. Your nerves are under strain while your sensitivity rhythm is surging from low into high. Beware of confusion and absentmindedness. Look both ways before you cross the street. With your intellectual curve down, think a little harder."

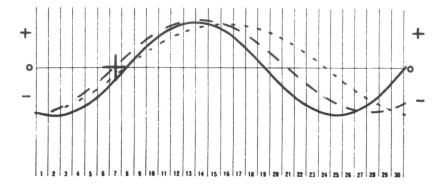

*Fig. 23-A:* Captain Gordon Eastridge, born December 14, 1931, crashed his Allegheny Convair 580 Airliner on June 7, 1971, when he made a too low approach in reduced visibility at the Tweed—New Haven airport. Twenty-nine of the 31 aboard were killed, including the pilot. His triple critical disposition could have been forecast by the IBM-360 biorhythm report which would have read as follows: "June 7, 1971 CAUTION. Hold on to the handrail. June 7th and 8th drag you through a critical 48 hours. First your nervous system will "poop" out, and then your physical energy will fade. Better postpone any important ventures and decisions. Intellectually also in critical so pretend you are helping yourself over a gangplank and take care not to slip."

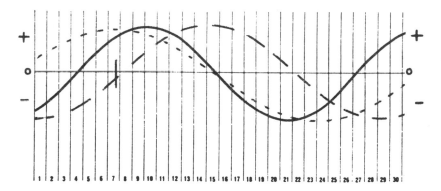

*Fig. 23-B:* First Officer James A. Walker, born March 2, 1937, who lost both legs in the crash, reported from the hospital that he momentarily considered wresting control of the plane, but decided it would be risky, improper, and unwise. Walker said that Eastridge was an excellent pilot, but on that morning, "It was different, it wasn't like him flying." Walker was on the eve of a critical off-day according to his chart.

*56*

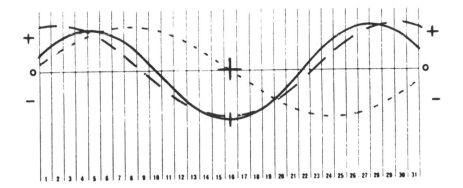

*Fig. 24:* Captain Don Jonz, born September 17, 1934, piloted the Cessna C110C in which he, with Congressman Hale Boggs, Nick Begich, and Russell L. Brown disappeared after takeoff from Anchorage, Alaska, on October 16, 1972.

News reports claim the aircraft carried neither locator transmitter nor survival gear. The biorhythm chart shows that on that day, Jonz was bottom low both physically and mentally, while his intellectual rhythm was critical. A dangerous day to undertake a precarious, ill-equipped mission.

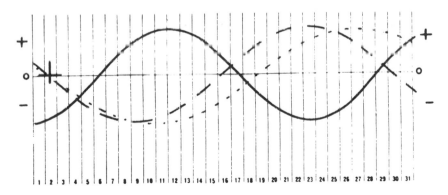

*Fig. 25:* Seeve R. Borowski, born May 14, 1948, flying a rented new Cessna, crashed into a grove of trees and was killed on March 2, 1973. NTSB investigator stated the weather was clear and there was no engine failure, but the aircraft was out of control. The biorhythm chart reveals the student's double critical in the mental and intellectual rhythms.

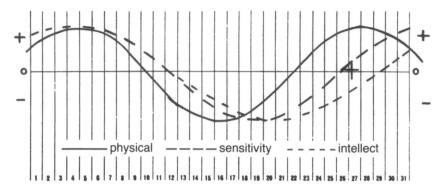

——————— physical   — — — — sensitivity   - - - - - intellect

*Fig. 26:* Pilot Captain Z. A. van Zanten, born February 5, 1927, was in a critical period on March 27, 1977, when his KLM 747 crashed into a Pan-Am 747 at Tenerife airport.

signs such as "slow down," "sharp curve ahead," and "slippery when wet" cause accidents rather than assure greater safety.

Safety in crowded skies is a major factor frightening passengers, especially so because a high percentage of tragedies are traced to human error. When KLM pilot Van Zanten took off in heavy fog at Tenerife Airport and smashed his KLM 747 into a Pan-Am 747, which had just landed on the same runway, the lives of 577 passengers were snuffed out in seconds. This experienced pilot evidently paid no attention to garbled dispatch signals and normal caution he should have used under such difficult conditions. Review of the tragic crash, under the direction of Prof. Sigmund Kardas at the University of Tenerife, established clearly that Van Zanten was in "critical" biorhythm disposition, aggravated by jet lag, language misunderstanding, and almost zero visibility. It is reasonable to believe that had he known his unfortunate biorhythm disposition, the tragedy would have been avoided.

## HOW TO CALCULATE BIORHYTHM

The procedure in biorhythm mathematics is to add up the total number of days in an individual's life, from the day of birth to the first day of the particular month for which a chart is desired. After this total is determined, it must be divided by 23, 28, and 33, the respective lengths of the three rhythms. These divisions will indicate how many times each cycle has run a complete span of 23, 28, and 33 days respectively; the remainders show the position of each rhythm on the first day of the month to be charted. The process is simple—but tedious—arithmetic; modern biorhythm aids avoid these calculations. However, since the charting techniques originated in this way, it is desirable to review this method of biorhythmic calculation in order to understand the system thoroughly. The detailed explanation that follows will serve as a simple demonstration for those who may suspect some mystical numbers must be used to make events correspond with biorhythm mathematics.

To make the explanation as clear as possible, let's take a specific example—a person born on Wednesday, August 5, 1942—and work out the calculations for the three biorhythmic cycles for October 1, 1986, proceeding as follows:


From August 5, 1942 to August 5, 1986.
44 years of 365 days ..................... 16,060 days
Extra leap-year days ......................... 11 days
From August 5, 1986 up to and including
October 1, 1986 as follows.
August .... 27 days
September . . 30 days
October ... <u>1 day</u>
          58 days...................... <u>58 days</u>
                                    16,129 days


This person lived a total of 16,129 days from his birthday on August 5, 1942 up to and including October 1, 1986.

In order to obtain the rhythm position for the October, 1986, chart, divide the total of days lived by the 23-day, 28-day, and 33-day rhythm units. The aim is to eliminate all completed rhythm units in order to discover the exact position of each rhythm as of October 1, 1986. These divisions result in the following:

16,129 divided by 23 equals 701 completed cycles
*plus 6 days.*
16,129 divided by 28 equals 576 completed cycles
*plus 1 day.*
16,129 divided by 33 equals 488 completed cycles
*plus 25 days.*

These calculations show that this person's October, 1986, chart starts with the 23-day physical rhythm on its sixth day. The 28-day emotional cycle starts with the first day at one on the chart. The 33-day intellectual cycle will be at its twenty-fifth day on the chart. The interpretation of the numbers 6, 1, and 25 is as follows: the 23-day physical rhythm is in high, the 28-day emotional rhythm starts a new upswing—a "critical" day—and the 33-day intellectual rhythm is at a low.

By preparing your own biorhythm charts, you will soon understand how each day forms a different composition of your life's patterns, showing your ups and downs, and alerting you to the few but important "caution" days during which you should watch your step.

## A SIMPLIFIED CALCULATING METHOD

Interest in biorhythm studies was greatly accelerated by the introduction of a series of calculation tables, which I added to the book *Biorhythm* by Hans Wernli, when it was translated into English. As technical supervisor for the American edition, I agreed with the publishers that these tables would help to reduce skepticism, since they would allow the reader to retrace each case documented in the book. They also offered the reader an opportunity to chart his own biorhythm and those of his family and friends. Three tables were included, each with specific and related key values. These same tables are shown in detail in Chapter 9 of this book.

The application of the calculation tables might best be described as triangular calculation. Table A shows a number for each day of a year for each rhythm. These numbers correspond to every possible birthday in a year. Table B shows a complementary number for each year, from 1887 to 2000; these numbers apply to the year of birth. By combining the numbers in Tables A and B for any given date, the basic birth date figures can be established. These figures, once established, do not change for that person; they are used in all future calculations. In order to chart the cycles for a given month, the numbers in Table C are merely added to the basic figures. Using the same birth date as in the previous example, August 5, 1942, proceed as follows:

|  | Physical 23-day Rhythm | Sensitivity 28-day Rhythm | Intellectual 33-day Rhythm |
|---|---|---|---|
| Table A: August 5 | 15 | 9 | 16 |
| Table B: 1942 | 0 | 25 | 24 |
|  | 15 | 34 | 40 |
| If any of the totals is greater than 23, 28, or 33 respectively, then deduct. | (23) | 28 | 33 |
| If smaller, carry down as is. | 15 | 6 | 7 |

These are the *basic figures* for the birth date of August 5, 1942, selected for this example. These numbers—15, 6, and 7— can be used throughout the life of this person in conjunction with any of the figures listed in Table C, as shown below. In other words, the basic figures from the combination of Tables A and B are fixed values in this method of calculating. By adding the third units from Table C, the final position of each rhythm, as of the first day of the month selected for charting, can be obtained.

To complete this example, use the rhythm figures for October, 1986, from Table C, and proceed as follows:

|  | Physical 23-day Rhythm | Sensitivity 28-day Rhythm | Intellectual 33-day Rhythm |
|---|---|---|---|
| Basic birth date, figures, as already shown. | 15 | 6 | 7 |
| Table C figures for October, 1986. | 14 | 23 | 18 |
|  | 29 | 29 | 25 |
| Again deduct 23, 28, or 33, respectively, when the totals are greater than these three figures. | 23 | 28 | (33) |
| If smaller, carry down as is. Final net figures used for charting October, 1986. | 6 | 1 | 25 |

These final figures—6 for the physical rhythm, 1 for the sensitivity rhythm, and 25 for the intellectual rhythm—are identical with those arrived at by the full mathematical calculation explained previously. It is evident that using the tables not only saves time and effort but also reduces the chance of making mistakes.

# 5

# PRACTICE IN BIORHYTHM STUDIES

## PROOF: PROFOUND AND SIMPLE

Since the original work by Swoboda, Fliess, Schlieper, and Teltscher, and the subsequent research by Schwing, Bochow, Tope, and Anderson, firmly established the tenets of biorhythmic theory, a number of recent discoveries have added further evidence to confirm the same mathematical rhythms in life. In addition, accident and death statistics, as well as the results of athletic contests, seem to give still further confirmation to the theory. As already mentioned, it is a known but unpublicized fact that some of the municipal systems abroad use biorhythm mathematics in accident analysis, like the study documented in Tope's report for the Sanitation Department of the City of Hannover in Germany. Such research is made especially to find out whether human error was the cause or a contributing factor, and who was at fault. A number of coaches of athletic teams, as well as many individual athletes, especially bicycle riders, have applied biorhythm to their training and competitions. All these statistics and reports substantiate Swoboda and Fliess's theory that, throughout nature, life flows in a regulated rhythmical pattern, creating the fluctuations man has come to recognize as his ups and downs. Birth and death, as well as man's changing moods and disposition, follow this regulated pattern.

In the medical field there is the statement made by Dr. F. Wehrli of Locarno, Switzerland, in the preface of the book *Bio-*

*rhythm,* in which he testified that he has used biorhythm mathematics in his hospital for over fifteen years, mostly to ascertain the best days for elective surgery; he has performed over 10,000 operations without a single failure or complication. In cases where no account is taken of biorhythmic cycles, statistics show that complications arise in from 30 to 60 percent of the cases.

Dr. Wehrli's statement aroused considerable interest among members of the medical profession in the United States. A statistical report covering twenty-eight operations performed at a New York hospital was submitted to me by an anesthetist. This was confidential information, the source of which I am not permitted to reveal. Analysis by biorhythm charting disclosed that nine out of these twenty-eight operations had been performed on critical days of the patient. After the mathematical biorhythm charts had been studied by the anesthetist, he informed me that three of these nine patients had died. Perhaps the list had purposely included these deaths because he had been as astounded by them as he later was by their correlation with the biorhythm analysis. I learned afterward that the death rate in operations averages only one in 5,000 to 6,000.

Unfortunately, this pilot investigation was not pursued further.

A few years ago, my work in biorhythm studies came to the attention of P. A. Costin, C.D., and O.St.S., M.D., Regional Surgeon, Quebec Medical Region, and Consultant Medical Director for the World Exhibition in Montreal in 1967. Dr. Costin has been interested in the cyclical behavior of man for many years, and his research has disclosed a striking similarity with biorhythm mathematics.

During our meeting in Montreal in 1961 I was given the opportunity to explain to Dr. Costin the use of the calculation tables, and I left a master-calculation book with him. I am most grateful for being allowed to quote from a letter from him in reference to the manuscript for the previous edition of this book:

Dear George:
From a short preview of your forthcoming book: "Is This Your Day?" I am delighted at this new contribution to the advancement of the research in life cycles. You have made it

easy for all to observe the obvious, even where most are inclined to deny it.

For some years now, I have used your calculations and your charts with success. Time and again, with the accuracy of correct data, I have obtained accurate results in the prediction of death in terminal cases of cancer, and in preventing accidents by advising the accident-prone; even the attempts at sex-determination of a forthcoming child have been surprisingly correct in most cases.

The proof of these life cycles is at this time in the obvious results observed; but the obvious is the most difficult to prove. I hope that your new book will help orient some new project of research in the biochemical field and that shortly a bright scientist will come forward with the scientific answer. In the meantime, I am satisfied with the validity of life cycles from the many cases I have observed and charted during the past few years.

Your pioneering in this field should be recognized at large with your new book, and I wish you all the success you so much deserve.

Yours sincerely,

*(signed)* Phil Costin

After reviewing the new research I had prepared for this edition, Dr. Costin wrote me:

Dear George:

During the past years, we have often discussed the considerable number of charts concerning war heroes, casualties of the Korean war, aviation accidents, car accidents and so many occurrences. We can only shrug an answer that the observations of past events support the validity of biorhythm and that the prospective value is surely there for those who are ready to heed to preventive warnings and evaluate them.

Your missionary work in relation to biorhythm will be greatly enhanced by the advantages of the IBM-360 computer print-out system which is exact and well formalized. Obviously nobody any longer denies the existence of man's genetic clock, although no one knows what makes it tick. Is the answer within the domain of molecular biology, cancer research?

*Fig. 27-A:* A Defensive Driving class with the teacher explaining the biorhythm theory and how students can draw their own charts.

*Fig. 27-B:* Japanese edition of *Is This Your Day?*

More scientists should ask questions about the uncanny accuracy and it may at last result in the hypothesis of research which will produce the scientific explanation. So far, I can only continue to wonder about the accumulation of ''observed'' facts and to believe that someone will come soon with explained facts.

With warm regards,
*(signed)* P. A. COSTIN, M.D.

## JAPAN GOING ALL OUT FOR BIORHYTHM

The introduction of a calculating system with my first hardcover edition, and later with the paperback, brought thousands of testimonial letters even from faraway countries. It is gratifying to report that many of these readers were anxious to reveal experiences in their own lives. Some would explain in detail how pre-knowledge of their biorhythm had saved them from accidents and how events in their daily life correlated perfectly with their biorhythm charts.

From such biorhythm enthusiasts evolved a group of men composed of insurance executives, doctors, and safety engineers who formed the Japan Biorhythm Association in Tokyo. After conclusion of their own research, an agreement was made to translate my book into the Japanese language for publication in Tokyo. Within a few years, transportation and trucking companies, taxi fleet operators and insurance companies initiated safety methods based on the biorhythm theory which resulted in reductions of from 35 to 45 percent of accidents and substantial savings in property damage claims.

Mr. Yujiro Shirai, the leading exponent of the Japan Biorhythm Association, sent me a review of their activities, from which I quote:

Your book *Is This Your Day?* which I translated, was chosen and recommended by the Japan Library Association. I am pleased to report that within only a few years, over five thousand firms have started using the biorhythm theory based on the mathematical background you initiated. Some plants include all employees, while others chart only the workshop group to improve safety and production efficiency. Of considerable influence were the traffic accident and death statistics prepared by the Tokyo Metropolitan Police and Traffic Department, followed by similar studies made in Osaka, Guma, Shiga, Hokkaido, Kyoto and other prefectures. Some of the research statistics were printed and distributed by traffic safety associations, and the biorhythm theory is now part of defensive driving courses offered all over Japan.

To mention only a few of the thousands of concerns using the biorhythm charts now prepared with small computer programmed printers are: Hitachi's Manufacturing Company, Fuji Heavy Industries, Asahi Glass, Mitsubishi Heavy Industry, Bridgestone Tire, Tokyo, Chubu, and Tohoku Electric Companies. Among the insurance companies are the Tokyo Marine and Fire, Yasuda Fire, Taisho Fire and Japan Fire Insurance companies, also Mitsui Life, Meiji Life, Asahi Life, and Fukoku Life. Some of the transportation companies are the Japan Express, Seino Transport, the Yamato Transport, as well as the International Automobile and the Odakyu Taxi Cab companies.

One of the Japanese transportation companies, operating 385 buses and 300 taxis, reported a reduction of from 35 to 40 percent in accident claims. Their safety engineer told the press that with the biorhythm charts, their men can keep tabs on their emotional changes and this has helped make their operators nicer persons and safer drivers.

It may be interesting for you to know the working methods we introduced in various plants.

1. Each person receives or makes his own chart.

2. Some plants place the biorhythm charts in the pay envelope.

3. Workers whose charts forecast a critical day receive warning slips advising extra caution on that day.

The instructions and working methods vary with the size and type of organization. For instance, some of the bus and taxi companies hand out little paper cranes (the crane is the

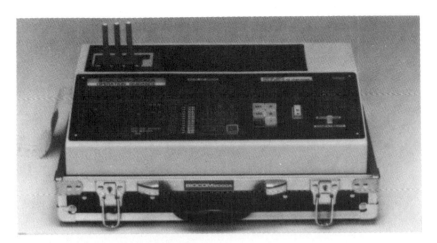

*Fig. 28-A:* Computer and biorhythm chart printer used by transportation systems and by insurance companies in Japan.

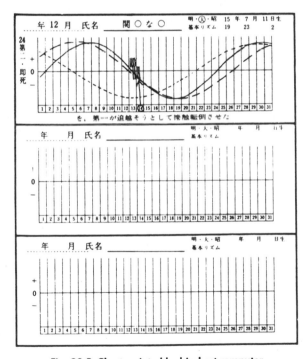

*Fig. 28-B:* Charts printed by biochart computer.

symbol of good luck and happiness) in different colors to each driver. The colors indicate their biorhythm condition. For the motorcyclists delivering mail and telegrams, small triangular flags in different colors are used, and another taxi company gives each driver a small empty caramel box. If the driver returns from his work tour and had no accident, the empty box is exchanged for a full one to bring home to his family.

These and other methods have helped the Nagahama Transportation division of the Omi Railroad to establish an accident-free record covering over four million kilometers. The Meiji Bread Company was able to reduce its yearly vehicle accident loss by 45 percent, saving about three and one half million yen, compared with the years preceding the introduction of the biorhythm theory for their drivers.

The Seibu Transport Company, after initiating the biorhythm system, assigned computer punch card operators to different jobs on critical days. This method reduced mistakes by 35 percent. The interest and application of our computer-programmed biorhythm charts is growing rapidly. The automobile division of large fire and marine insurance companies such as the Tokyo Marine, Yasuda Fire, and Taisho Marine and Fire, have started a biorhythm program, using the charts also for canvassing new prospects. Their success proved so rewarding that I believe the system will soon be adopted in an extensive way.

The biorhythm theory instruction courses we originated in cooperation with the Traffic Department of the Police appear to produce a new, safety-conscious generation of drivers in Japan. The Shiga and the Gumma Prefecture Traffic Safety Associations are now issuing monthly biorhythm charts to 250,000 drivers. Not to be left out, the Nissan Motor Corporation, one of the largest automobile manufacturers in Japan, gave away free biorhythm charts to all visitors. This proved a great attraction during the introduction of their new models in their five largest, most important showrooms.

Yours very sincerely,
*(Signed)* YUJIRO SHIRAI, Representative
The Japan Biorhythm Association

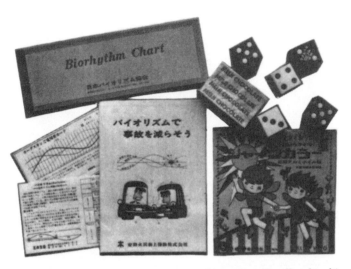

*Fig. 29-A:* Biorhythm Chart folder, instructions and incentive gifts offered to drivers.

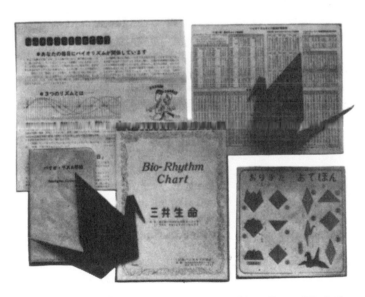

*Fig. 29-B:* Biorhythm Chart handbook and calculation tables, gifts, and biorhythm calendar used by industry and insurance companies.

In the United States, the interest in biorhythm has grown on its own merits and through person-to-person recommendation. Our way of life, our thinking, and to a great extent our reactions to new ideas seem to follow the trend of wanting things "prepackaged" and "instant." Mathematics, to many, is a time-consuming and painful experience they'd rather leave to machines. Even after having learned how to calculate and draw one's biorhythm charts correctly, the interpretation of the day-to-day changes in the sine-curves present difficulties many of the do-it-yourself biorhythm enthusiasts loathe. To solve this obstacle, I carefully studied the tens of thousands of variations in the biorhythm pattern over the span of a lifetime and prepared a detailed text with interpretation of a 644-day span of the combined 23-day physical and 28-day emotional rhythms. Calibrated calendar rulers make it easy to date the program for 644 days and for years in advance. This Bio-calendar is available from Bio-calendar, Inc., P.O. Box 66509, St. Petersburg Beach, FL 33736.

## WHY DO ATHLETES BREAK RECORDS?

Every so often newscasters and sportswriters tell of a new record being made by an athlete, and then again, of an unexpected failure by the same champion. We naturally wonder why, and what could have happened. A striking example of an apparent change in athletic ability is the performance turned in by golfer Arnold Palmer. During the first week of July, 1962, Palmer started off with a 67-stroke qualifying round for the British Open at Troon, Scotland. He continued in top form, winning the title with a total score of 276, four strokes ahead of his nearest rival. During this tournament, Palmer established all kinds of records and sailed through each day with the greatest of ease. Even the liveliest gallery could not shake him. His physical condition showed no strain—although he had complained of a sore back—and, in fact, he told a UPI sports writer that the heat (about which others were complaining) was doing him good.

Mentally, Palmer was Mr. Pleasant, smiling at the large and

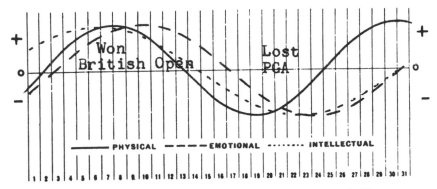

*Fig. 30:* Arnold Palmer, born September 10, 1929, won the British Open Golf Tournament during a triple high period in July, 1962. Two weeks later, during the following triple low, he lost the P.G.A. Tournament.

pressing crowd. He used good judgment in distance and in picking the right club for each shot. His biorhythm chart for this early part of July, 1962, shows Palmer in a long, triple high period. Such situations exist only about every five months, when the three cycles line up together in the upper portion of the graph.

Palmer immediately flew back to New York, and then in his own airplane to Newton Square, Pennsylvania, in order to get in a few practice rounds before the coveted Professional Golfers' Association championship would start. Everyone expected him to win hands-down, but he was in an unfortunate biorhythmic position, with all three rhythms in a low or recuperative period. Biorhythmically speaking, he met his Waterloo; as often happens in overtrained and overstrained men, there was no reserve power left. Though the spectators gathered early in anticipation of a characteristic rally, Palmer was unable to produce and ended up tied for seventeenth place, ten strokes behind Gary Player.

The Associated Press report on July 21, 1962 carried the headline: "Is Pressure Getting Too Much for Palmer?" A New York newspaper noted: "Arnie Shows His Anger"; evidently he became angry at the spectators crowding in on him, something he had seemed to enjoy ten days before in Scotland. Lincoln A. Werden of the *New York Times* reported that Palmer was at the clubhouse well ahead of late contenders, saying that he was mentally tired.

A logical question is: Could Palmer have overcome his difficulties at Newton Square? The chances are that he could have avoided overtaxing his physical, mental, and intellectual capabilities by taking it easy, instead of pushing himself by doing extra practice rounds. Had he known his negative biorhythmic condition, he could have steeled himself for the occasion.

This case is not an isolated one; in July, 1961, Palmer also lost the P.G.A. title when both his sensitivity and intellectual rhythms were in low position.

Baseball might be a fertile field for verifying pitchers' and batters' performances and potential, except that it is a team sport and often more than one player determines the outcome of a situation. However, a biorhythmically informed coach could anticipate the possible slump of an opposing pitcher. He could also save his own pitchers or batters by using them sparingly on critical days. The critical day of a player who has already shown a proneness toward accidents should signal a special warning. On May 18, 1962, Mickey Mantle hit a hard drive, and as he was rushing toward first base, suddenly collapsed. His biorhythmic position, high physically but critical in sensitivity, was typical of high accident affinity, which seems to result from too much strength in relation to coordi-

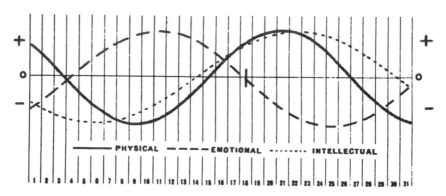

*Fig. 31:* Mickey Mantle was born October 30, 1931. On May 18, 1962, after hitting a hard drive, he suddenly collapsed during the run to first base. The biorhythm chart for this month shows that May 18 was a critical day in his sensitivity cycle; both the physical and intellectual cycles were high.

nation and nerve reaction—matter over mind, to turn a phrase.

An ardent baseball fan and devotee of biorhythm mathematics sent me a carefully prepared review of Mantle's biorhythmic positions. He had diligently noted Mantle's performance each day on the bottom of the Bio-Charts, and pointed out how closely this corresponded with the conditions shown on the charts. If the explanation of the mathematical background of biorhythm induces other readers to undertake such research, the results may prove most rewarding.

## NO-HIT PITCHING

An interesting study was sent to me by an ardent baseball fan, Robert R. Hambley, who operates the Lakeview Computer System at St. Petersburg, Florida. He wrote: "There seem to be a number of places where biorhythm should be taken into account when planning one's activities. It's a shame more people don't." Hambley enclosed the computer-programmed biorhythm charts of four no-hit games pitched by Sandy Koufax in 1962, 1963, 1964, and 1965, and seven by the pitchers Jack Kralick in 1962, Juan Marichal in 1963, Bob Lemon in 1948, Don Larson in 1956, Cy Young in 1897, and John VanDermer in 1938.

Of these eleven no-hit games, nine coincided with a critical day of the pitcher, most of them with the physical switching down. Could this indicate that on such days these pitchers were so charged up they disregarded all caution? Does this thought lead to explain why such days often show up in accident cases?

Performance studies of other athletes, when correlated with their biorhythmic disposition, are just as revealing.

Students of psychology may wonder whether several successive defeats might not influence a champion's outlook to the point where he feared defeat before he started. As in the case of an illness or injury, time will heal. But if an athlete is aware of his own negative biorhythmic position, he is better equipped to overcome defeatism or fear because knowledge of the reason for a defeat can act as a tonic.

*75*

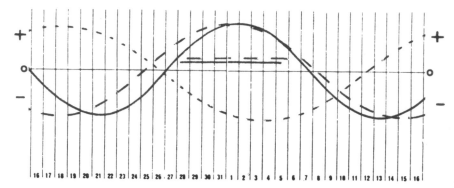

| 16 | 17 | 18 | 19 | 20 | 21 | 22 | 23 | 24 | 25 | 26 | 27 | 28 | 29 | 30 | 31 | 1 | 2 | 3 | 4 | 5 | 6 | 7 | 8 | 9 | 10 | 11 | 12 | 13 | 14 | 15 | 16 |

*Fig. 32:* **Mark Spitz, born February 10, 1950. Olympic superstar won seven gold medals and set new swimming records. His performance during one week is unequaled in the history of modern Olympics. Mark Spitz was favored by the high period in both his physical and emotional rhythms during the end of August into September, 1972, at Munich.**

Victories or defeats do not always admit of such clear-cut analysis; often, a number of outside circumstances have to be taken into consideration. At times, the biorhythmic condition may act only as a subtle influence with some people, but it can become a decisive factor under other conditions. Self-observation is probably the best and the most interesting approach. In this connection I quote from a letter I received from Eddie Lane of Columbus, Ohio, a radio sportscaster who kept close track of the performance of the famous Ohio State University basketball team:

I have traveled with and broadcast the games of the Ohio State basketball team for two years, and during that period I had the entire team charted. It was always quite evident from their charts as to how they were going to perform, and their performance always coincided with the charts.

Out of curiosity I made my own chart for the month of December 1956. On the 13th of that month I had a succession of upsetting events and wound up the day having a head-on accident with another car. Two people were hospitalized but fortunately no one was killed. My chart showed I had a critical day in both the physical and the sensitivity rhythm and also was low in the intellectual rhythm.

76

I have never known anything that can give more help to a person if they will intelligently use it.

On April 7, 1963, the *San Diego Union,* San Diego, carried a half-page article by Jerry Magee under the headline: "Girl Scientist Charts Prep Five on Biorhythm Theory." The story relates how Myra Logerwell, a La Jolla High School freshman, became interested in biorhythm charting when her mother fell while rushing to answer the phone, and broke several ribs. Myra calculated the biorhythm chart and found her mother had had a critical day in all three cycles. This test case so convinced her that she undertook her own research. She charted the basketball team and also recorded various events that proved to her the subtle influences of biorhythms could be verified. Her study and presentation won Myra a first prize in the medical science division of the Greater San Diego Science Fair. It also won her a special award in the psychology division.

An acquaintance informed me that a careful study of twenty-five of his employees, who were doing creative art work, taught him to be more understanding of his people. At first—that was several years ago—he prepared the biorhythm charts of his staff six months in advance and locked them up in his safe. At the end of this trial period, he compared the charts with the records he had noted in his diary from day to day, and found that performances tallied with the biorhythm charts. Convinced, now, that biorhythm mathematics reveal in a large measure what goes on inside us, he prepares his work assignments to correspond with the biorhythm forecast for his staff.

## VICTIMS OF MENTAL IMBALANCE

We often use the expression: "He lost his head!" and ask ourselves, what made him or her do it? Reviews of crimes where sudden impulse appeared to have driven someone to commit murder, or where a person committed suicide after enjoying success and apparent happiness, often put the blame on the phase of the moon or the use of drugs or alcohol. Pursuing my special interest in the biorhythm theory and hoping to find a biological answer based on

77

mathematics, I charted numerous cases and review a few which are nationally known and where the facts, dates, and the mathematics leave no doubt as to their accuracy. Some of the most striking cases were in connection with the exposed public lives of the Kennedy brothers and people in the entertainment world.

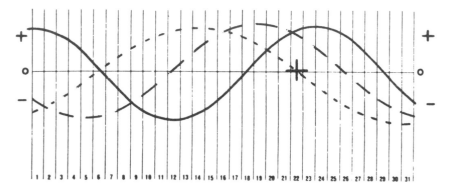

*Fig. 33-A:* The late President John F. Kennedy, born May 29, 1917, drove through Dallas on November 22, 1963, in a triumphant procession. He was physically and emotionally at his best. However, his intellectual rhythm registered "critical." Could this disturbing element in clear thinking have caused him to disregard the safety of the bulletproof bubble top on the car which could have saved him from the assassin's rifle shot?

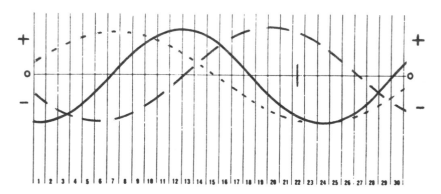

*Fig. 33-B:* Lee Harvey Oswald, born October 18, 1939, had planned and practiced on rifle ranges for his crime well in advance. For him, it was only a question of when the opportunity would present itself to shoot Kennedy. Oswald's highly charged mental state may have assisted his perfect coordination.

78

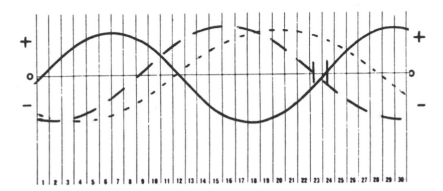

*Fig. 33-C:* Jack Ruby Rubinstein, born March 11, 1911, evidently was deeply affected by the tragic assassination of his idol. After a disturbing critical in his emotional rhythm on November 23, 1963, he must have decided to take the law in his own hands and he went to the jail in the basement and shot Oswald point blank, as two sheriffs were leading the alleged assassin to the courtroom. November 24, 1963, was a critical day in Ruby's physical rhythm.

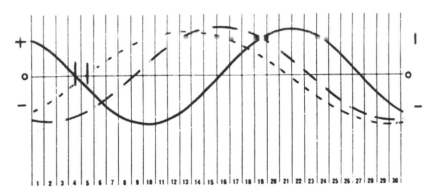

*Fig. 34:* Sirhan B. Sirhan was born in Jerusalem, March 19, 1944. Amid cheers and flashing V-for-victory signs, Senator Robert F. Kennedy had just moved into an anteroom of the Hotel Ambassador on June 4 to 5, 1968, when shots were fired, wounding the senator critically. The assassin's biorhythm chart pinpoints the double critical state that probably triggered his madness.

*79*

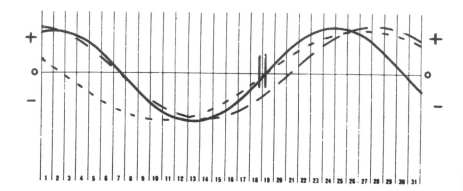

*Fig. 35:* Senator Edward M. Kennedy, born February 22, 1932. On July 18, 1969, Kennedy was driving his twenty-eight-year-old secretary Mary Jo Kopechne to the Edgartown Ferry slip to catch the last boat. However, instead of turning left on Main Street, he drove to the right into an unpaved road leading to a deserted beach.

According to newspaper reports, his car scraped eight yards of the wooden guard of a narrow bridge and somersaulted into ten feet of tidewater.

This tragic accident took a life and shocked the nation. The senator, apparently dazed, did not report the accident until nine hours later. His biorhythm chart clearly reveals the precarious critical in his physical and intellectual rhythms with a low emotional curve.

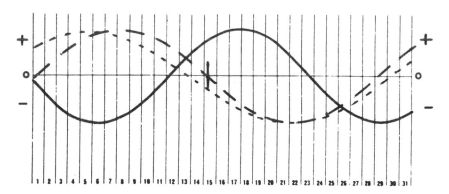

*Fig. 36:* Arthur H. Bremer, born August 21, 1950. On May 15, 1972, Bremer pushed himself through a crowd applauding Alabama Governor George Wallace and shot him point blank. The mentally disturbed disposition of the criminal is shown in Bremer's critical state on that day.

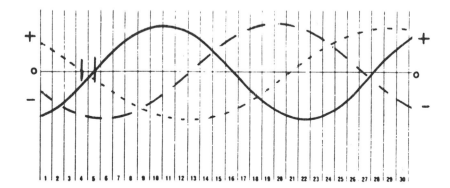

*Fig. 37-A:* Marilyn Monroe, born June 1, 1926. The queen of Hollywood's pin-up stars took an overdose of sleeping pills during the night of June 4 to 5, 1961. Fortunately she was found and revived in time to save her life. The critical position of both the intellectual and the physical rhythm combined with a depressed state in her sensitivity cycle are shown in her biorhythm chart.

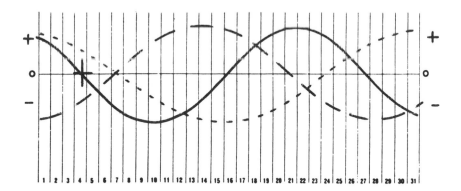

*Fig. 37-B:* On August 5, 1962, Marilyn was found dead in her bed after another bout with drugs. A critical day in her physical rhythm coincided with her wish to end it all.

*81*

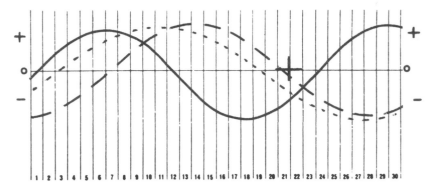

*Fig. 38:* Judy Garland, born June 10, 1922. Her rainbow had ended when she was found dead in the bathroom of her London home on Sunday morning, June 22, 1969. An overdose of medication during the night, when her emotional rhythm was at a critical point, could have influenced her action. She was also physically and intellectually in low gear.

## MENTAL CONCENTRATION AND GAMES

Readers who wonder why they lost that poker game in spite of a promising hand, or others who unexpectedly conquered a formidable chess opponent, may find at least a partial answer in biorhythm mathematics.

Applying biorhythm mathematics to the performance of Bobby Fischer during the 1962/63 world championship matches reveals considerable evidence of the operation of biorhythm. In one respect, Fischer might consider himself lucky that the matches were held during a period which for him was exceptionally favorable.

All three of his biorhythms—physical, emotional, and intellectual—were high most of the time, and two of his *potentially* critical days were "no play" days for Fischer. It is interesting to speculate what he might have scored had the matches been held two weeks before, when he was in a complete low in all cycles.

Since chess is a test of mental skill rather than a physical strain (anyone who has just completed a tournament may disagree), the 28-day sensitivity rhythm and the 33-day intellectual rhythm can be considered the most important.

The first match, which took place on December 17, ended in a draw on the eve of Fischer's first critical biorhythmic day. Fischer suffered a loss on December 18, a critical in his sensitivity rhythm. It must have been a disappointing start, but it was Fischer's only loss during the entire championship—and also the only critical day he experienced during the tournament.

On December 20 he registered a win, but the next day he again had a little trouble, obtaining a draw only, when he had a critical in the intellectual rhythm. A win, another draw, and two more wins followed on December 26 and 27. On December 28, a critical in his physical rhythm, the schedule-makers unwittingly favored him by making it a "no play" day. January 1, New Year's Day, which would have been a critical in Fischer's sensitivity rhythm, again was "no play," and he finished the championship with a win on January 3.

Fischer's pattern of win, draw, or loss suggests that biorhythm may provide an insight into the vagaries of performance. The application of biorhythm mathematics in the world of games could be quite meaningful. A player, knowing that his biorhythm was unfavorable, need not give up a match, however. The human mind and body are flexible enough so that one can compensate when aware of adverse conditions.

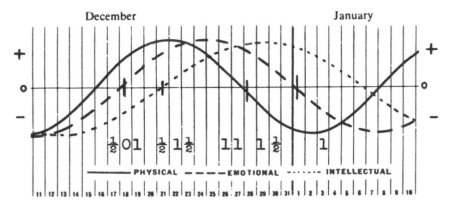

Fig. 39: Bobby Fischer, born March 9, 1943, registered his only loss during the 1962/63 chess championship on a critical day in his sensitivity rhythm, December 18, 1962.

# 6

## BIRTH—THE MOMENT OF TRUTH

The investigators whose work resulted in the concepts of biorhythm mathematics concluded, from their studies, that on the day of birth all three major human biorhythmic cycles start off together. Subsequent experience has confirmed their conclusion. Therefore, in order to obtain accurate results, the individual must know the correct date of his birth.

To the skeptic, this apparent verdict of experience will serve only to raise the fundamental question: *Why* is the day of birth in every case the true starting point? After all, the skeptic will remind us, the event of birth varies enormously from case to case. Some infants come into the world on greased skids, so to speak, after a short and uneventful maternal labor, but others are delivered only after prolonged and even exhausting ordeals. Still others do not pass through the birth canal at all but are literally lifted out of their mothers by Caesarean operation, the timing of which may have little to do with the precise time when delivery would normally have occurred.

Most infants are born about nine months after conception, but some arrive as much as several weeks later and others are born prematurely after six to eight months. (The Parke-Davis gestation chart used by pediatricians figures 40 weeks—280 days—counting from the last day of menses to the term of birth and allowing seven days each side of that date.) These so-called premature babies usu-

*84*

ally survive only through extraordinary medical measures and special care. Furthermore, if biological rhythms are at work in the infant before birth, as seems to be inferable from the evidence of embryology and obstetrics, is it reasonable to assert that these rhythms must suddenly be "reset" to their starting points at birth, regardless of their particular values and phase relationship just before birth?

To answer these questions, let's consider what actually happens at birth, regardless of the time or circumstances, if the infant survives. It is quite clear that whether the delivery occurs at term or is premature, after an easy or a difficult labor, with or without medical or surgical aids, two very striking events must befall every infant at the time of birth: first, a massive stimulation of all the sensory organs and of the nervous system, and second, sudden and drastic changes in virtually all the vital functions. At no subsequent time in life will the individual experience such profound and rapid readjustment. The mother's uterus is comfortably and constantly warm, dark, and relatively silent, and here the unborn infant's body floats weightlessly in a fluid medium of constant composition. There is no need for it to move from one place to another to escape discomfort or pain; there are no hunger pangs or thirst.

At birth, this parasite's paradise comes to an abrupt end. Suddenly it is colder. The body is squeezed and pushed and pulled, perhaps slapped to encourage breathing. Air abruptly enters the lungs, drying and chilling the delicate membranes. The body has weight; bright lights and harsh sounds stab through the tender flesh. The world seemingly has come to an end. No wonder the infant cries!

Even as it emits the first yell of protest, profound changes are under way in its body. The most striking are those that result from the separation of the infant from the mother's bloodstream. During life in the uterus, the umbilical cord has carried the unborn infant's blood to and from the placenta, an organ attached to the inside lining of the uterine wall. This permits the mother's bloodstream to supply food, water, and oxygen to the bloodstream of the infant, and to remove from it waste products, including carbon dioxide.

As soon as the infant is born and the umbilical cord is severed, all the functions performed by the placenta must be taken over by the infant's own organs. The burden of excreting waste products from the blood falls on the kidneys, the lungs have to absorb oxygen and eliminate carbon dioxide, and the flow of blood through the heart must be rerouted so that all the blood entering the right half of the heart goes entirely through the lungs and is then returned to the left half of the heart for distribution to the rest of the body.

As one authority has written: "However complicated are the circulatory readjustments needed for postnatal life, and however prolonged the interval until their complete accomplishment, a period of only three hours or less normally elapses before the human circulation behaves like that of an adult in terms of the distribution of oxygenated blood."[5]

It is clear, therefore, that the birth process and the hours immediately after birth are truly a new beginning, a new point of departure for virtually every organ in the body. It would be most remarkable, indeed, if the vital rhythms of the body remained unaffected by such climactic events.

## IDENTICAL RHYTHMS IN DIFFERENT PEOPLE

The mathematical regularity of biorhythm is inflexible, and therefore people born on the same day have the same biorhythm throughout their lives. This statement may sound questionable if interpreted to mean that all people who are born on the same day will encounter the same "fate," as some may term their future. Life, fortunately, does not appear to be that simple. Inherited traits, health, character, education, work, and, of course, circumstances vary so much that any degree of similarity is considered quite remarkable.

Biologically, our chance of having exactly the same chro-

[5]Clement A. Smith, *The Physiology of the Newborn Infant,* 2nd ed., 1951, C. C. Thomas, Springfield, Ill. Quoted in J. P. Greenhill, *Obstetrics,* 11th ed., 1955, W. B. Saunders Co., Philadelphia, page 55.

mosome inheritance as someone else is one in billions. Even identical twins, the offspring of a single ovum, although alike in their inherited chromosome arrangement, must develop differently. Psychiatrists report that approximately 40 percent of man's character is inherited and 60 percent is developed on the basis of outside influences.

The Philadelphia Inquirer carried an article by Dr. Ernest G. Osborne on March 2, 1963, under the heading: "All Children Have Inborn Difference," in which he states that those who watch babies in the nursery of a maternity ward will notice how each one differs from the others, and not just in outward appearance. Some will lie quietly; others are constantly on the move. Some are alert to sound or light. There are other differences too. We recognize that the way infants are handled, even at this early stage of life, seems to have a profound effect on the kind of human beings they become, but their inborn differences are equally influential, not only in infancy but throughout life.

We learn from such specialists that practical experience confirms the existence of enormous differences in human beings from the very start of their independent and natural lives. Thus, although the biological clocks or the biorhythms of those born on the same day may tick off in identical patterns, each life follows a separate path.

For each person, a different relative combination of the three rhythms appears each day. The five-day variation between the length of the 23-day, the 28-day, and the 33-day rhythms mathematically permits the repetition of an identical combination only after a lapse of 58 years and 67 or 68 days, depending upon the number of leap years. This is arrived at by multiplying 23 by 28 by 33, which gives 21,252 days. Of course people born 21,252 days apart will have the same biorhythm, but the process of aging, which in itself follows a rhythmical pattern of duplicate biorhythms, creates an entirely different situation for the older person.

Another, and more interesting, repetitive pattern is created by the 23-day physical and 28-day sensitivity rhythms, which mathematically join for a new simultaneous start every 644 days, approximately every year and nine months. This interval is often referred to as the biorhythmic year. Its possible significance will be more fully explained in Chapter 7.

## A BOY OR A GIRL?

*Can Biorhythm Predict Sex?*

Man's rhythmic cycles, as already explained, influence many of the ordinary things he does and thinks and feels each day. A necessary question is: Do these rhythms of life have an influence on the miracle of birth?

Researchers, intrigued by such a possibility, began drawing charts to discover whether any connection existed between biorhythm, birth, and the sex of babies. They figured that since the event of giving birth is, for the mother, a physiological shock, the circumstances brought about by a critical day might help to induce labor and thus start the process of birth. According to studies already completed, their assumption was correct; a surprisingly large number of babies are born on the mother's physical or emotional critical day. Because there are many other possible influences that may induce labor, and because the process of conception, gestation, and birth is such a complex chain of events, births do not always occur precisely on schedule, and therefore no one should expect to be able to make predictions with anything close to 100 percent accuracy. But there have been enough successful predictions to make such planning interesting and useful.

If determining the time of birth on the basis of biorhythm seems intriguing, determining the sex of the unborn child is positively fascinating. Relying on such predictions may seem almost outlandishly naive, and might actually be so, except for the fact that there has been a startlingly high record of successes.

In arriving at a method for making a forecast, two recognized biological facts must be kept in mind:

(1) The sex of the child is determined at the moment of conception.

(2) The sex is determined by the male, since it depends entirely on whether the ovum is fertilized by an X (female) or a Y (male) sperm cell.

One additional factor must be understood in order to recognize the relationship of biorhythm and sex determination. Biologists usually state that chance alone decides whether an X or Y sperm cell happens to reach the egg first and fertilize it. Another theory, however, suggests that the egg may at certain times be more predisposed to accept the X cell, and at other times the Y cell. Thus, although the first sperm cell reaching the egg can produce fertilization, the one that is accepted by the egg may depend on some female physical factor at that particular time.

Biorhythmically, it is suggested that when the physical cycle is high *in the mother* at the time of conception, the egg is predisposed toward accepting Y cells, and thus eventually produces a male child. Similarly, if the emotional cycle is high in the mother during conception, biorhythmists suggest there is a reasonably good chance she will give birth to a girl. The reason behind these probabilities is that a high physical (23-day) rhythm favors a condition of alkalinity in the blood, whereas a high sensitivity (28-day) rhythm tends to create a condition of acidity.

To illustrate how these predictions are arrived at, let's consider the birth of Viscount David Linley, born November 3, 1961 to Princess Margaret. The Princess's biorhythm chart for October-November, 1961 discloses that the child was born right after a critical day in her 23-day physical cycle. Her obstetrician, knowing approximately when she was due, could have pinpointed the date of birth by using biorhythmic theory, which would have shown in advance when her critical days would occur.

The sex of a child apparently depends on the approximate date of conception. This can be determined by counting back 280 days, the normal gestation period; in the case of Princess Margaret, conception would have occurred toward the end of January, 1961, as shown by the chart in Fig. 40-B.

The chart indicates that she was high in the 23-day physical cycle during the probable period of conception, between January 24 and 26. This may seem merely a coincidence. Acceptable proof of sex determination will result only from the analysis of thousands of cases. But to make this case somewhat more believable, let's check the biorhythm chart when Princess Margaret gave birth to her "dream" baby girl on May 1, 1964. Here again birth occurred close to a critical periodic day, this time in the 28-day emotional rhythm. Going back 280 days to July 24 and 25, 1963, reveals that she was in a high or plus phase in the 28-day emotional rhythm at the time of conception, indicating favorable prospects for a girl.

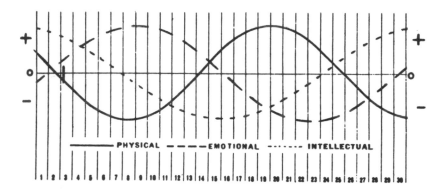

*Fig. 40-A:* Princess Margaret, born August 21, 1930, gave birth to a baby boy on November 3, 1961, at the end of a critical day in her physical rhythm.

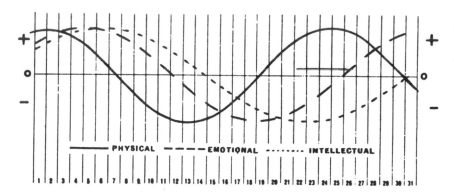

*Fig. 40-B:* Princess Margaret's biorhythm chart for January, 1961, shows her high in the physical rhythm during the probable days of conception, January 24/25.

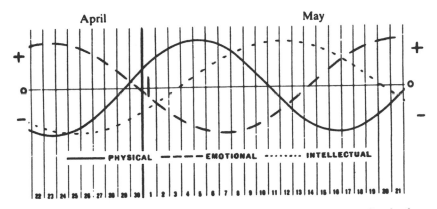

April                  May

PHYSICAL ————EMOTIONAL ········ INTELLECTUAL

*Fig. 41-A:* Princess Margaret gave birth to a baby girl on May 1, 1964, immediately after a critical day in her sensitivity cycle.

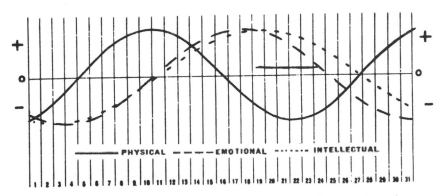

PHYSICAL ————EMOTIONAL ······ INTELLECTUAL

*Fig. 41-B:* Princess Margaret's biorhythm chart for July, 1963, shows her in high sensitivity position during the probable days of conception.

Any reader who wants to perform the calculations necessary to "predict" the sex of an offspring may find it simpler to arrive at the day of expectance by adding a year to the probable date of conception, and deducting 85 days.

For a reverse example: In the case of Princess Margaret's second child, we may add 85 days to the birth date of May 1, 1964. (We add 30 days additional for May, 30 for June, and 25 for July, totaling 85.) Projecting back to 1963 gives the date of July 25, 1963.

The biorhythm hypothesis, as noted, suggests that if ovulation occurs during a plus or high period in the 28-day emotional cycle, a condition is created favorable for the attraction of a female-type (X) sperm cell. Whether this phenomenon *is* created by a predominantly higher condition of acidity or alkalinity, [6] or by differentials in the electromagnetic field, should provide an interesting project.

Some guidance is offered by a device used abroad that creates a positive or negative electromagnetic field and thereby attracts either male or female sperm cells. This device, coupled with artificial insemination, has been used to predetermine the gender of herds and flocks. [7]

The proud father of a boy or a girl may therefore have no more to do with determining the sex of his child than contributing the ample millions of sperm cells needed to stimulate the hormones required for conception. [8]

In my own research, I have found many cases in which I was able to predict the sex of an unborn child by the use of the biorhythmic theory. When, during conception, the mother was clearly in a high phase in the 28-day (sensitivity) cycle, she would give birth to a girl; if she were in a high phase in the 23-day (physical) rhythm, she would give birth to a boy. There are cases, however, in which conception takes place when both these cycles are either up or down simultaneously, and then a clear-cut prediction is not possible.

[6] "Can You Choose the Sex of Your Child?" Article by Dr. Irving C. Fischer, Assistant Professor, New York Medical College, as told to Joseph Kaye. *Ladies' Home Journal,* February, 1962.

"Name It and You Can Have It!" Article by John Troan, reviewing report by Prof. Jean Bourgeois-Pichat, director of the National Institute of Demographic Studies in Paris. *New York World-Telegram and Sun,* December 28, 1963.

[7] "We Have More than Five Senses." Article by Leonard Wallace Robinson, reporting on the Barnard-Russian experiments. *New York Times Magazine,* March 15, 1964.

[8] "New Advances in Female Fertility." Articles by Isbelle Taves on research by Prof. Carl Genzell of the National School University of Uppsala, Sweden. *Look Magazine,* May 19, 1964.

One case with which I am familiar probably is similar to many others. A couple with two daughters were anxious to produce a boy. Knowing about the biorhythm theory, they had their biorhythm charts prepared. For conception, they chose a clear high in her 23-day physical cycle during the ovulation period, and became the parents of the boy they had hoped for.

## DOES BIORHYTHM LEAD TO FATALISM?

Reading about the discovery of the three cyclical patterns, the subsequent documentation, and the biological and mathematical explanations of the regularity of biorhythms can lead a person to the point of either rejecting the theory or being willing to follow it a step farther. The next step after reading is doing, for only by his own observations can an individual gain insight into himself, his changing feelings, his impulses and affinities. With a reasonable measure of application, a person soon recognizes his good days and his bad days. But this measure of predictability in no way interferes with free will!

Most people are concerned about their safety and about understanding life with its changing patterns. The often-used expression, "I wish I had known," indicates that foresight is considered a valuable asset—especially so after one has suffered an accident, made a bad decision, or failed to forestall an unfortunate event. On the other hand, there are people who live with the idea that everything happens as it must, and that their fate is quite thoroughly predetermined in every detail. Such people often close their eyes to indications that might warn them of potential danger or an unpleasant experience. Fatalism—the blind submission to events—has slowed progress throughout history; man's advances are largely the result of curiosity and analytical thinking. The protective warnings of possible danger experienced by our primitive ancestors may have had much to do with man's survival through the ages.

People today generally believe in insuring themselves against losses by accident, death, fire, theft, and all manner of risks, which past experience shows may lurk just around the corner. Constructive, realistic thinking and the planning of activities in the light of a knowledge of one's ups and downs are simply a type of self-insurance. Charting his biorhythm cycles provides a person with a subtle warning of days when his disposition is potentially critical; the more mature a person is, the more important this knowledge can be. Children trip, fall, and get hurt often, but youth is flexible, tough, and heals fast.

Accidents generally become less frequent when the child grows into an adult, and are usually most serious in old age. Discussing accident statistics during a White House interview in January, 1961, Doris Mersdorf, National Safety Council specialist, pointed out that persons over sixty-five account for 28 percent of the accidental deaths and 20 percent of all disabling injuries. Significantly, the old-age group represents only 9 percent of our population, and so this accident ratio is alarming.

The documentary background and statistics in this book are included to prove two points: first, that life does actually follow a regulated and rhythmical path; second, that biorhythm can help forecast the subtle influences that may affect man's disposition and capabilities. Such advance indications are *not* designed to predict accidents, human error, or a person's fate, but only—and quite specifically—to suggest that during approximately 20 percent of his days, when under trying outside influences or circumstances, a person is in a more dangerous situation than at other times.

For the elderly, the facts disclosed by the National Safety Council should weigh heavily in favor of the precautionary warnings offered by a knowledge of biorhythm. It is relatively simple to note the few days each month when one's affinity for human error is most pronounced.

# 7

# BIORHYTHM AND SOCIOLOGY

## A STUDY IN COMPATIBILITY

Biorhythmic relationships were closely studied by Swoboda and Fliess, who collected hundreds of family trees to demonstrate a cyclical pattern of births from one generation to the next. These studies were also pursued by Schlieper, Schwing, and others interested in human behavior. Many reports have been published in Germany and Switzerland pointing to a higher degree of compatibility in couples with similar or at least close biorhythmic dispositions. For instance, people whose 23-day and 28-day biorhythmic cycles pulsate in similar rhythms were found to be more compatible than those whose rhythms were out of step with each other. A report made in connection with a study of assembly-line workers in a factory making precision parts indicated that when groups of workers with similar biorhythmic disposition worked together, a more harmonious situation prevailed and resulted in better work and fewer rejections.

Although the full impact and the practical application of such studies are problematical, it should be interesting if not revealing for individuals to study their biorhythmic compatibility with their marriage partner, friends, teammates, and business associates. Understandably, people with similar physical and sensitivity dispositions will appreciate physical and mental challenges at the same time and therefore tend to get along better.

Hugo Max Gross, in his book *Biorhythmik, Das Auf und Ab Unserer Lebenskraft* (Biorhythm, the Ups and Downs in Our Lives),* devoted several chapters to explaining rhythm relationship in connection with marriage, partnership, teamwork, and other sociological situations. A condition of 100 percent biorhythmic compatibility in all three rhythms would result from having the same birth date. There are, however, many variations that bring the three rhythms at least close together; in the case of the 23-day physical and 28-day sensitivity rhythms, any multiple of 644 days brings them into complete harmony.

In terms of percentages, the 23-day rhythm changes 8.7 percent with each day of separation. The sensitivity rhythm of 28 days changes 7.1 percent per day, and the intellectual rhythm of 33 days changes 6 percent per day of separation. For example, in the physical rhythm, one day apart between two people would bring the compatibility percentage to 91.3 percent; two days apart, to 82.6 percent; three days, to 73.9 percent, and so on down to the halfway mark at 11½ days, which indicates the exact opposite position, registering zero as a compatibility factor. From then on, the compatibility percentage rises again at the rate of 8.7 percent each day until the 23rd day, when the 100 percent status is reached again.

The 28-day sensitivity rhythm, starting at 100 percent, reaches the zero compatibility point on the 14th day and then climbs up again to reach 100 percent on the 28th day of this cycle. These daily percentage changes in each of the three rhythms are shown in the following table. All one has to do is figure out the number of days apart two or more people are in each of the three rhythms, and then read the respective percentage in compatibility from the table. To find the composite biorhythm compatibility factor, add the percentage for each rhythm and divide by three.

## HOW TO FIND THE COMPATIBILITY PERCENTAGE

The calculations necessary to find the percentage of biorhythmic compatibility between two people are fairly simple. First, compare the basic birth-date figures (the totals of the Tables A and

*96*

B) or the figures for the current month. The idea is to find out how many days apart each rhythm is from the same rhythm of the other person. Once the difference in days apart has been established, the percentage can be read from the Compatibility Table.

For example, John Doe, born January 6, 1926, and Mary Doe, born November 16, 1928, would calculate their biorthythm compatibility as follows:

|  | | *John Doe* | | | | *Mary Doe* | | |
|---|---|---|---|---|---|---|---|---|
| Born: Jan. 6, 1926: | Table A | 19 | 24 | 29 | Nov. 16, 1928: | 4 | 18 | 12 |
| | Table B | 2 | 17 | 27 | | 7 | 14 | 22 |
| | | 21 | 41 | 56 | | 11 | 32 | 34 |

Deduct any completed cycles;

| if smaller, carry down as is: | 23 | 28 | 33 | | 23 | 28 | 33 |
|---|---|---|---|---|---|---|---|
| | 21 | 13 | 23 | | 11 | 4 | 1 |

| Basic birth-date figures for John Doe: | 21 | 13 | 23 |
|---|---|---|---|
| Basic birth-date figures for Mary Doe: | 11 | 4 | 1 |

Deduct the smaller figures from the larger to arrive
at the number of days apart ....................   10   9  22

Consult the Compatibility Table for the respective percentage values, as follows:

10 days apart in the 23-day rhythm = 13% compatibility
9 days apart in the 28-day rhythm = 36% compatibility
22 days apart in the 33-day rhythm = 33% compatibility

Composite total = 82

To arrive at the average compatibility of John and Mary Doe, divide the composite total of the three percentages by three (82 ÷ 3); this shows their compatibility average to be 27.3 percent. The two charts show clearly how differently the three rhythms run between these two people.

The 27.3 percent compatibility of this couple is a comparatively low average, and they are bound to find their reactions

*97*

## COMPATIBILITY TABLE

| 23-Day Rhythm | | 28-Day Rhythm | | 33-Day Rhythm | |
|---|---|---|---|---|---|
| Days Apart | Percentage Change | Days Apart | Percentage Change | Days Apart | Percentage Change |
| 0 | 100% | 0 | 100% | 0 | 100% |
| 1 | 91.3 | 1 | 93 | 1 | 94 |
| 2 | 82.6 | 2 | 86 | 2 | 88 |
| 3 | 73.9 | 3 | 79 | 3 | 82 |
| 4 | 65.2 | 4 | 71 | 4 | 76 |
| 5 | 56.5 | 5 | 64 | 5 | 70 |
| 6 | 47.8 | 6 | 57 | 6 | 64 |
| 7 | 39.1 | 7 | 50 | 7 | 58 |
| 8 | 30.4 | 8 | 43 | 8 | 52 |
| 9 | 21.7 | 9 | 36 | 9 | 46 |
| 10 | 13 | 10 | 29 | 10 | 39 |
| 11 | 4.3 | 11 | 21 | 11 | 33 |
| 11½ | 0 | 12 | 14 | 12 | 27 |
| 12 | 4.3 | 13 | 7 | 13 | 21 |
| 13 | 13 | 14 | 0 | 14 | 15 |
| 14 | 21.7 | 15 | 7 | 15 | 9 |
| 15 | 30.4 | 16 | 14 | 16 | 3 |
| 16 | 39.1 | 17 | 21 | 16½ | 0 |
| 17 | 47.8 | 18 | 29 | 17 | 3 |
| 18 | 56.5 | 19 | 36 | 18 | 9 |
| 19 | 65.2 | 20 | 43 | 19 | 15 |
| 20 | 73.9 | 21 | 50 | 20 | 21 |
| 21 | 82.6 | 22 | 57 | 21 | 27 |
| 22 | 91.3 | 23 | 64 | 22 | 33 |
| 23 | 100 | 24 | 71 | 23 | 39 |
| | | 25 | 79 | 24 | 46 |
| | | 26 | 86 | 25 | 52 |
| | | 27 | 93 | 26 | 58 |
| | | 28 | 100 | 27 | 64 |
| | | | | 28 | 70 |
| | | | | 29 | 76 |
| | | | | 30 | 82 |
| | | | | 31 | 88 |
| | | | | 32 | 94 |
| | | | | 33 | 100 |

NOTE: *The percentages in the 28-Day and 33-Day columns are expressed in the nearest whole number.*

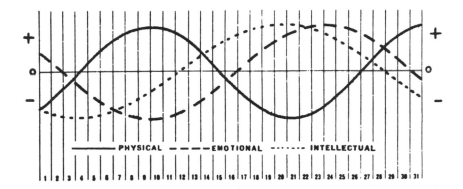

*Fig. 42-A and 42-B:* The low compatibility factor is clearly apparent in these charts. The three rhythms fluctuate almost in opposite cycles.

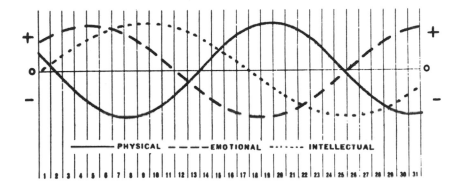

and feelings often at variance—but their general character will also have an effect. Unfortunately, this mathematical compatibility factor or relationship will never change—their mutual ups and downs always will remain "locked."

What will help this couple—and all like them—is a great deal of understanding, an ability to forgive and forget easily, not to mention a healthy dose of affection and love.

In contrast to this low compatibility factor, here are the calculations for Bill Smith, born the same day as John Doe, January 6, 1926, and Helen Smith, born July 17, 1929.

|  |  | *Bill Smith* |  |  | *Helen Smith* |  |  |
|---|---|---|---|---|---|---|---|
| Born: Jan. 6, 1926: | Table A | 19 24 29 | July 17, 1929: | 11 | 0 | 2 |
|  | Table B | 2 17 27 |  | 10 | 13 | 20 |
|  |  | 21 41 56 |  | 21 | 13 | 22 |
| Deduct any completed cycles; |  |  |  |  |  |  |
| if smaller, carry down as is: |  | 23 28 33 |  | 23 | 28 | 33 |
|  |  | 21 13 23 |  | 21 | 13 | 22 |

Basic birth-date figures for Bill Smith:      21  13  23
Basic birth-date figures for Helen Smith:     21  13  22

Days apart . . . . . . . . . . . . . . . . . . . . . . .      0   0   1

Here the picture is entirely different. Expressed in biorhythm compatibility percentages, this combination works out as follows:

0 days apart in the 23-day rhythm = 100% compatibility
0 days apart in the 28-day rhythm = 100% compatibility
1  day apart in the 33-day rhythm =   94% compatibility

Composite total = 294

Dividing the total by three gives an average compatibility of 98 percent.

The biorhythm charts for this couple clearly show the harmonious fluctuations of their rhythms.

This second example shows an unusually high compatibility factor of 98. Generally, an average of 60 or better is considered good. In studying the biorhythm compatibility theory closely, it is important to evaluate each rhythm percentage separately. A high percentage of compatibility in the 23-day physical rhythm is of importance to people who engage in team sports, or to those who lead an active physical life. It means that their high and low periods will come during approximately the same days. Some of the football teams in Europe are making use of this knowledge, arranging their starting lineups in order to obtain the best performance. Key players are used sparingly during their off days in order to save their energy.

The 28-day rhythm, accredited to nerve reaction and to sen-

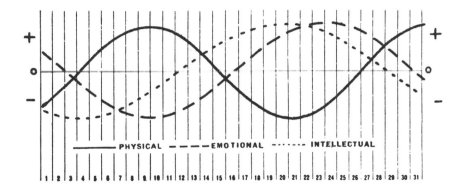

Figs. 43-A and 43-B: The high compatibility factor shown in these charts is obvious. The three rhythms follow almost identical patterns.

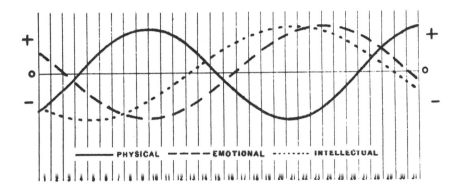

sitivity, is probably the most important rhythm to be observed by married people and in family life. Young children especially reflect changes in this rhythm, a fact that was first observed by Swoboda. He often advised young mothers not to worry if their babies refused food during their critical days of the 28-day rhythm. During the early stages of life, he maintained, a baby's system simply cannot absorb the regular amount of food because other developments of a cyclical nature seem to disturb life's "chemical factory."

Sensitivity, feelings, and emotion play an important part also in older people. Later in life, when the honeymoon is over, respect and devotion are important for a successful marriage or partnership.

When people grow older, they are less inclined to give in, firmer in following their own intuition and feelings. A clear understanding of a husband or wife's biorhythmic disposition will help in anticipating those trying days when things may most easily flare up.

Since the 33-day rhythm reflects the changing tides of man's intellect, his capacity to absorb new subjects and to remember, it has only a minor influence on his capacity to get along with others. The most valuable aspect of the biorhythm compatibility study is the insight it gives friends, partners, and couples into their inner feelings and dispositions. Recognizing and being able to anticipate these changes is the first step in intelligent advance planning for a harmonious relationship.

A high degree of biorhythmic compatibility, however, is no foolproof assurance that two people will get along perfectly all the time. Nor can the opposite be assumed of people with a low degree of biorhythmic compatibility. The effect of these subtle influences is bound to vary with each person's general character and temperament, and also with what happens to him from day to day. The fact remains, though, that most people experience a higher degree of attachment to certain particular relatives, friends, and associates than to others. A close study of this phenomenon through biorhythm mathematics might be an interesting contribution to human understanding.

The examples given so far were prepared to show how biorhythm compatibility can be figured out on the basis of the Tables A and B. Compatibility can also be obtained by comparing the calculations for any current month—the totals of the Tables A, B, and C. This comparison, however, *must be based on the same month* for any couple or group of people involved.

You, the reader, can easily ascertain your compatibility percentage and average factor with your husband, wife, partners, and friends by following these instructions. Such knowledge may not only give you an insight into your good—and your trying—days, it will also grant you the knowledge to guide your family and business life through physical and emotional storms because you can prepare for them well in advance.

# 8

# DOES BIORHYTHM INFLUENCE
# THE COURSE OF LIFE?

## CRITICAL DAYS—A SIGNAL FOR HEART ATTACKS?

Analyses of deaths caused by heart attacks cover considerable ground. The results quite generally lend additional confirmation to the theory that man's biorhythms are highly regulated. Heart attacks are not always fatal, and death does not always strike on critical biorhythmic days; however, there seems to be sufficient correlation to encourage a broad and impartial investigation.

A person with a heart condition may find comfort and some peace of mind in knowing in advance the days when extra care, rest, or precaution is advisable. Medical reports indicate that about 65 percent of those who suffer heart attacks survive the attacks and are generally able to live a full life if they take the necessary precautions. It appears analogous that it is as wise for a person to be aware of the subtle tides of life as it is meaningful for the captain of a ship to know the reefs and the shoals at low tide.

One of the impressive heart-attack cases I had occasion to precalculate was the death of Clark Gable on November 16, 1960. As a guest on radio station WOR, I was interviewed by Long John Nebel and his panel of writers and psychologists. This was on November 11, 1960, five days before Gable's death. During our discussion of biorhythm I was asked to draw Gable's biorhythm chart for November, 1960, because he had suffered a heart attack on November 5—

*Fig. 44:* Clark Gable, born February 1, 1901, suffered his first heart attack during a double critical period on November 5, 1960, and passed away during the second attack on November 16, 1960. Both these dates are clearly indicated on his biorhythm chart.

from which he was recovering. The panel carefully followed my calculations. We found that Gable had experienced his first attack on a critical day in his 23-day physical cycle. Examining his biorhythm chart for the weeks ahead, I pointed out that November 16 *could* present another critical situation. On that day Gable's physical cycle would switch into the low phase, and on November 17-18 his 28-day sensitivity cycle would switch from low to high, creating successive critical days. Such a combination, I indicated, could present two difficult days during his recovery, although his doctors reported him to be doing well. In fact, his recovery had been so pronounced during his biorhythmic physical high that the heart machine, which evidently saved his life during his first attack, was taken away.

During this broadcast I expressed the hope that Gable would be watched most carefully during his next nearly double critical day, November 16, pointing out that according to biorhythm mathematics his affinity for a relapse or another attack was strong. Unfortunately, the great movie star was stricken again on that particular day, and subsequent news reports stated that doctors believed "Gable could have been saved had the heart machine been available quickly."

My statistical research covers hundreds of similar cases. They cannot be described as "scientifically" irrefutable, in the strict sense of the word, because research that is unquestionably acceptable by scientists or by the medical profession requires thousands of carefully controlled cases, recently observed in this country, and usually under the auspices of a recognized institution, organization, or foundation. Since I lack such support, this type of case material is not available to me, and as an individual devotee I cannot afford either the time or expense involved in such a project. However, I have no fear that the theory of biorhythm would be disproved by any such "acceptable" studies.

Let's consider a few additional heart-attack cases, using the biorhythm charts of men who are well known and whose history and birth dates are common knowledge. These cases are not presented to imply that the heart attacks, fatal or not, could have been predicted. The charts merely lend additional proof of the regularity of biorhythm cycles.

President Dwight D. Eisenhower, born on October 14, 1890, suffered a heart attack in Denver on November 26, 1957, when his 28-day sensitivity rhythm reached a critical day while both his 23-day physical and the 33-day intellectual rhythms were in low. Whether this heart attack was triggered by exhaustion, high altitude, or other influences, only medical men were in a position to judge. However, I made numerous charts of President Eisenhower's disposition during his active years, and they all fit perfectly into this rhythm pattern.

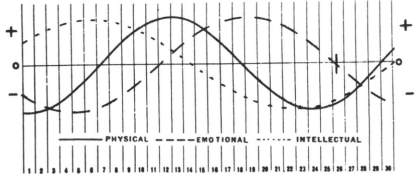

*Fig. 45-A:* President Dwight D. Eisenhower, born October 14, 1890, suffered a heart attack during a critical day in his sensitivity rhythm, with the physical and intellectual rhythms at low—November 26, 1957.

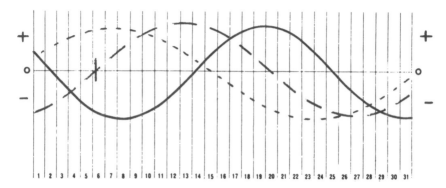

*Fig. 45-B:* President Dwight D. Eisenhower suffered five or six more heart attacks. A severe one which was headlined occurred on August 6, 1968, twelve hours after he had addressed the Republican National Convention in Miami Beach.

## CAN BIORHYTHM BE TRACED UNTIL DEATH?

The pages immediately following show the biorhythm charts of a number of well-known people for the month in which each died. Their birth dates, obtained from obituaries, are also given, so that the charts can be recalculated by anyone. These death statistics were chosen to lend additional documentation to the biorhythm theory, which claims that life follows a regulated pattern governed by the 23-day, 28-day, and 33-day rhythms, and that this pattern can be traced through human error and natural death. Students of biorhythm believe that as long as statistical research can trace these patterns backward in life, the same mathematical accuracy must be assumed to regulate life in the future, and that such predisposition can be a valuable tool in guiding daily living.

These cases were not selected to fit a pattern or a claim; rather, they represent a list of people famous enough so that their birth and death dates were easily available. No attempt has been made to find out which of the two important life rhythms is the more dominant one. Nor was any attempt made to find out whether it was the critical first day of a rhythm, or the halfway mark during the cycle when a rhythm switches into low, that was influential. It seems certain, however, that these critical days in life should receive close attention, especially in cases of illness.

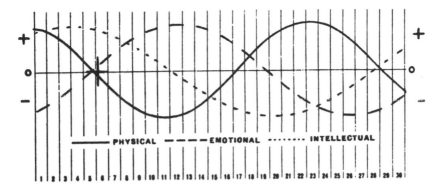

**Fig. 46:** Carl G. Jung, the world-famous psychoanalyst who created such terms as "introvert" and "extrovert," born on July 26, 1875, died during a double critical day, June 6, 1961.

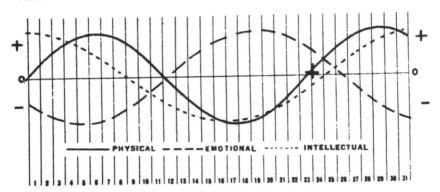

**Fig. 47:** Auguste Piccard, pioneer Swiss explorer of the stratosphere and the ocean depths, born January 28, 1884, died March 24, 1962. At the time of his death his physical rhythm was at the end of a low period.

**Fig. 48:** Jean Piccard, Auguste's twin brother, was also a noted balloonist and an aeronautical engineer; he died on his seventy-ninth birthday, January 28, 1963, when his biorhythm chart showed a double critical day.

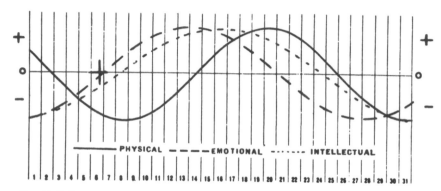

**Fig. 49:** William Faulkner, Nobel Prize—winning author, born September 25, 1897, died on July 6, 1962, of a heart attack. His biorhythm chart shows a critical day in his sensitivity rhythm.

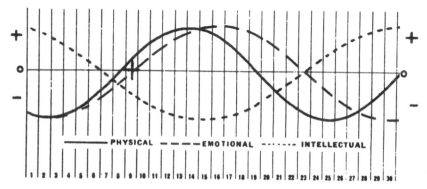

**Fig. 50:** Pat Rooney, one of the greatest song-and-dance stars of the vaudeville era, born July 4, 1880, passed away September 9, 1962. As can be seen from the biorhythm chart, Mr. Rooney experienced a physical critical the day before his death and was critical in sensitivity the day he died.

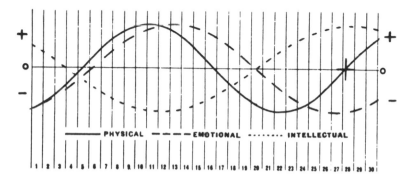

**Fig. 51:** Queen Mother Wilhelmina of the Netherlands, who reigned for over fifty years, was born August 31, 1880, and died November 28, 1962. She had been ill for several weeks; a heart disease speeded up the gradual deterioration of her state of health, and she died on a physical critical day.

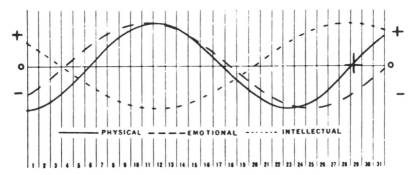

*Fig. 52:* Robert Frost, one of America's greatest poets, born March 26, 1875, expired on January 29, 1963; his physical rhythm was at a critical point.

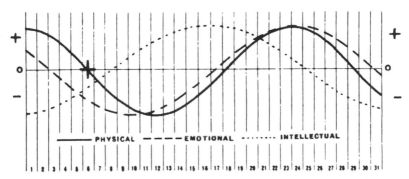

*Fig. 53:* Monty Woolley, stage and screen actor who was famous for his snow-white Van Dyke beard and his ability to play crotchety men with hearts of gold, was born on August 17, 1888, and died on May 6, 1963. His physical rhythm was in a critical position at that time.

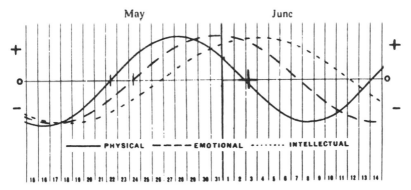

*Fig. 54:* On June 3, 1963, the world silently went into mourning over the death of Pope John XXIII. After a prolonged and valiant struggle, the Pope, who was born on November 25, 1881, finally succumbed. A week before, the religious leader had teetered on the brink of death, but he pulled through each new crisis with reassuring success. During this period of a week, the Pope was in a physical, emotional, and intellectual high phase; unfortunately, this high could not last indefinitely. The physical rhythm, in its sweep downward, reached a critical point between June 2 and 3, the day of the Pope's death.

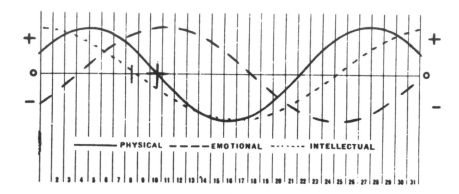

PHYSICAL ———EMOTIONAL ········ INTELLECTUAL

*Fig. 55:* Senator Estes Kefauver, the crusading Tennessee Democrat, born July 26, 1903, died on August 10, 1963, a critical day in his physical rhythm, while surgeons were preparing to operate on him at the Naval Hospital, Bethesda, Md. The Senator had been taken to the hospital two days before, after suffering a mild heart attack.

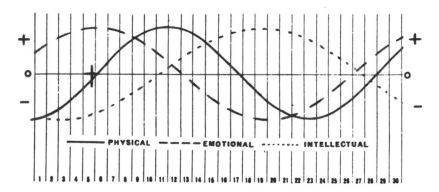

PHYSICAL ———EMOTIONAL ········ INTELLECTUAL

*Fig. 56:* General Douglas MacArthur, born January 26, 1880, died in the afternoon of April 5, 1964, after a determined fight for life. The general had undergone three operations, but life ebbed slowly until his physical rhythm came to the end of a cycle.

110

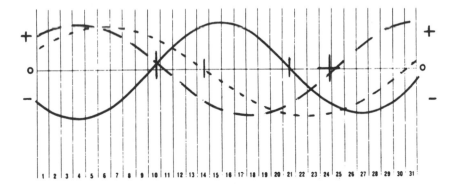

**Fig. 57:** Prime Minister Winston Churchill. On January 15, 1965, a medical bulletin from London revealed that Sir Winston had suffered a stroke and had slipped into a deep sleep. The day was a critical one in his intellectual rhythm, which according to my research seldom relates to heart attacks. This puzzle was solved later, when his physician reported that the stroke news was withheld for four days and that Sir Winston was actually felled on January 11, a critical day in his sensitivity rhythm, in fact a double critical condition. His pulse, it was reported, continued to flicker through the 21st, a critical day in his physical rhythm, and death came on January 24th, the end of his sensitivity rhythm.

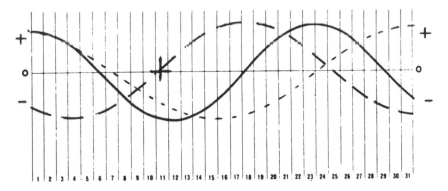

**Fig. 58:** Erle Stanley Gardner, born July 17, 1889. The mystery writer and creator of the Perry Mason show died at his home on March 11, 1970, a critical day in his sensitivity rhythm.

*111*

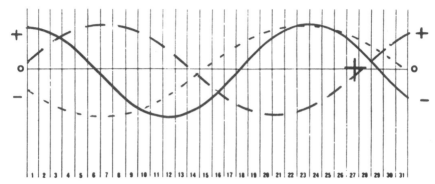

Fig. 59: Antonio de Oliviera Salazar, Portugal's dictator, born April 23, 1889, a peasant's son, he became the longest reigning dictator in modern European history. Suffering a head injury from a fall in September, 1968, Salazar's life gave out on July 27, 1970, at the end of his 28-day sensitivity rhythm.

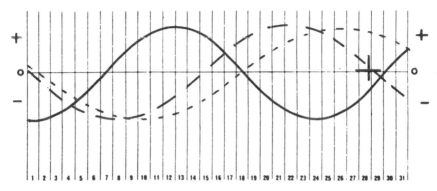

Fig. 60: Gamal Abdel Nasser succumbed to a heart attack on September 28, 1970. Nasser was born on January 15, 1918. At his death, his 28-day sensivity rhythm was breaking into low, a critical day disposition.

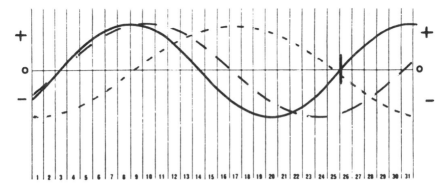

Fig. 61-A: J. C. Penney, born September 16, 1875. A man who parlayed a one-room dry goods store into the 1700-store retail chain, fell in his apartment on December 26, 1970, and broke his hip, a double critical day.—See next chart please.

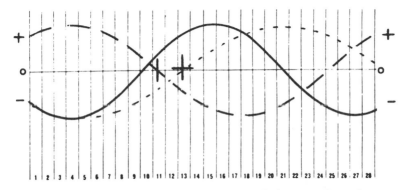

*Fig. 61-B:* J. C. Penney, born September 16, 1875. Suffered a heart attack on February 11, 1971, and died the following day.

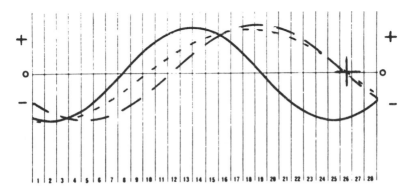

*Fig. 62:* "Fernandel." The great French comedian Fernand Joseph Desire Constantin, born May 8, 1903, died of lung cancer on February 26, 1971, a double critical day.

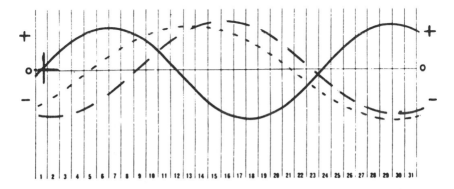

*Fig. 63:* J. Edgar Hoover, born January 1, 1895, died in his sleep Monday night, May 1, 1972. He had served his country as director of the F.B.I. for 48 years. His death coincided with a critical day in his physical rhythm.

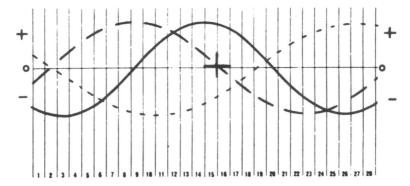

*Fig. 64:* Edgar Snow, born July 19, 1905, author on China, died in Lausanne after an operation on February 15–16, 1972, a critical day in his sensitivity rhythm.

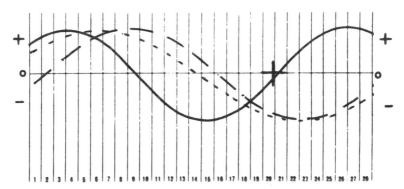

*Fig. 65:* Walter Winchell, born April 7, 1897, the "Let's go to press" news commentator, died of cancer February 20, 1972, a critical day in his physical rhythm.

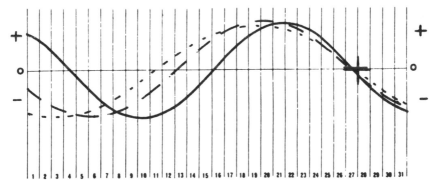

*Fig. 66:* The Duke of Windsor, born June 23, 1894. The former King Edward VIII of England died at 2:25 A.M. on May 28, 1972. He had just experienced a triple critical day.

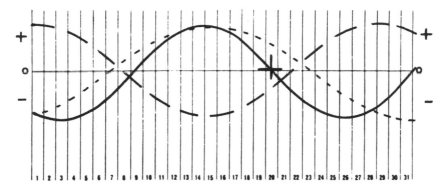

*Fig. 67:* Lester B. Pearson, Canadian Prime Minister, born April 23, 1897, died on December 20, 1972, a critical day in his physical rhythm.

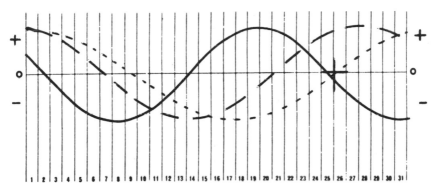

*Fig. 68:* Harry S Truman, former President, born May 8, 1884, after suffering kidney and heart complications died during a double critical day on December 26, 1972.

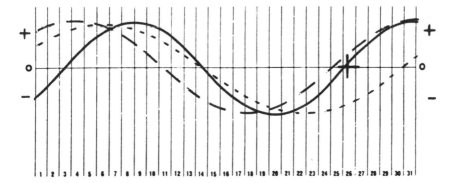

*Fig. 69:* Edward G. Robinson, born December 12, 1893, the "Little Caesar" of the movies, died on Friday, January 26, 1973, a critical day in his physical rhythm, preceded by a critical in his sensitivity rhythm. Robinson had suffered a heart attack on June 17, 1962.

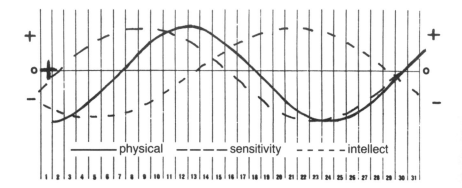

*Fig. 70:* **Rock Hudson (Roy Harold Scherer), born November 17, 1925, a Tuesday, died in his sleep October 1 to 2 (Tuesday-Wednesday), 1985. Hudson's intellectual rhythm was at a critical point, and his physical and sensitivity rhythms were low.**

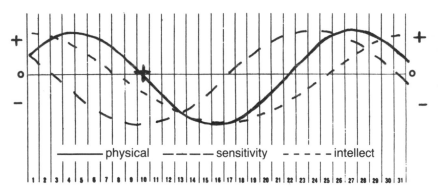

*Fig. 71:* **Orson Welles, born May 6, 1915, a Thursday, died of a heart attack on Thursday, October 10, 1985. He was experiencing a critical day in his physical rhythm, and his sensitivity rhythm was at a low.**

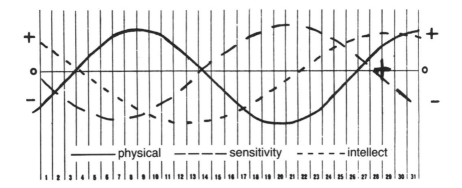

physical ————— sensitivity ----- intellect

| | 1 | 2 | 3 | 4 | 5 | 6 | 7 | 8 | 9 | 10 | 11 | 12 | 13 | 14 | 15 | 16 | 17 | 18 | 19 | 20 | 21 | 22 | 23 | 24 | 25 | 26 | 27 | 28 | 29 | 30 | 31 |

*Fig. 72:* Fred Waring, born Saturday, June 9, 1900, suffered a massive stroke on Saturday, July 28, 1984, and died on Sunday 1 A.M. Waring was at a critical point in his sensitivity rhythm on the day he suffered his fatal stroke.

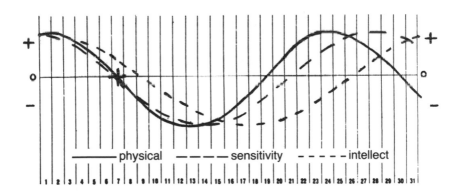

physical ————— sensitivity ----- intellect

| | 1 | 2 | 3 | 4 | 5 | 6 | 7 | 8 | 9 | 10 | 11 | 12 | 13 | 14 | 15 | 16 | 17 | 18 | 19 | 20 | 21 | 22 | 23 | 24 | 25 | 26 | 27 | 28 | 29 | 30 | 31 |

*Fig. 73:* Justice Potter Stewart, born Saturday, January 23, 1915, died after a stroke on a double critical day, December 7, 1985, a Saturday. His physical and sensitivity rhythms were both at critical points, a particularly hazardous combination.

117

# CONCLUSION

The claim that a person can predict how he will feel tomorrow—or at any stated time in the future—is something most people refuse to believe. Yet everyone has experienced happy or depressed days that seem to come from nowhere. Dr. Swoboda took great pains to explain that the philosophy of biorhythm accepts and confirms, rather than modifies, the law of periodicity in man. Nature, he declared, offers ample proof that the impressions a person receives from within form a highly organized pattern that has a profound influence on his actions and capabilities.

The idea that biorhythm may in some manner allow a person to recognize and even to foretell his capabilities and feelings may be frightening to those who are fatalists. Man, although adventurous and enterprising, usually fears that predictability would interfere with free choice. However, the realization that he does *not* have to be subjected to unpleasant events is bound to cheer even the eternal pessimist. Those who think realistically will welcome the opportunity of learning more about themselves through the simple application of biology and mathematics. Present knowledge of the biorhythm theory is not nearly complete or beyond intelligent doubt, but the studies and research that have been conducted over the last sixty years should at least challenge seekers for truth to investigate the field further. It is for this reason that I felt compelled to present the background and the mathematics clearly, and in a manner that would enable anyone to prove biorhythmic cycles do exist—to his own satisfaction, and perhaps that of his family and friends.

In this new edition, you'll find profound confirmation of the high sensitivity of our inborn life rhythm in relation to solar time, which is based on the earth's rotation. Even the State Department recognizes the effect of jet lag in long-distance travel, and the National Bureau of Standard confirms the stress imposed by one hour changes from standard time to daylight saving time in June, and back to standard in fall. Fortunately our biorhythms will adjust in a matter of days, and catch up with the sun, the basic time of all life on Earth. Let no critic tell you differently.

This book is written with my sincere wish to help you lead a fuller and safer life, by knowing the few days each month when you must avoid hasty decision, and take no chances. An ounce of prevention is worth a pound of cure should be your motto.

To facilitate such self-studies, it was decided to complete this book by extending the calculation tables as far in advance as 2008, and to include biorhythm chart blanks and print calibrated cycle rulers so that they might be cut out easily and used for practical testing of the theory. Additional biorhythm chart blanks and cycle rulers made in durable plastic, as well as other biorhythm aids, are available by writing to Bio-calendar, Inc., P. O. Box 66509, St. Petersburg Beach, FL 33736.

# 9

# HOW TO CALCULATE AND CHART YOUR DAYS

Tables A, B, and C, shown on the following pages, provide a short cut for figuring out how many days a person has lived since birth and where the three biorhythm cycles stand on the first day of the month for which a biorhythm chart is desired.

Table A refers to the *day* of birth and designates a number for each cycle for each day from January 1 to December 31.

Table B shows the numbers assigned to the *year* of birth from 1887 to 2000. By adding the numbers in Tables A and B for the day and year of birth, the *basic* biorhythm figures can be obtained for each of the three rhythms. These basic figures will not change during a person's life. They should be noted for future reference, because they can be used for calculating the final figures for any month shown in Table C.

Table C shows the relative numbers assigned to the first day of any *month* between January, 1982, and December, 2008. This table is used for the selected dates. It makes possible the calculation of a biorhythm chart for any month as far back as 1982 and as far forward as December, 2008. You can review past events, such as a victory or defeat in sports event, a self-caused accident, or a birth in the family, as well as investigate compatibility or sex-determination. You will also be able to draw biorhythm charts for months or even years ahead, and thereby be able to lead a fuller and safer life.

*120*

Make each necessary addition of the numbers shown in the tables a step at a time, and follow the example carefully, using your own birth-date numbers taken from Tables A and B. Then add the numbers shown in Table C for the month you wish to chart. The procedure is so quick and easy that it will be no trouble to chart your family and friends, or to discover why you yourself feel so energetic or are sunk in the doldrums. Your chart will also warn you when to watch your step and to be especially cautious in your driving.

Study the example thoroughly. Remember to make the *three* separate sets of calculations needed for the 23-day, 28-day, and 33-day rhythms. Remember, too, that the composite of the additions made using all three tables A, B, and C, is required to arrive at the correct rhythm position for the month selected for charting.

When drawing a biorhythm chart use RED (either pencil or ball-point pen) for the 23-day physical rhythm, BLUE for the 28-day sensitivity rhythm, and GREEN for the 33-day intellectual rhythm. These rhythms are shown in this text by a solid, interrupted, and dotted line respectively.

Now paste the calibrated cycle rulers onto stiff paper or thin, light-weight cardboard, and cut them out carefully. Locate the 23-day rhythm position number (the composite number from charts A, B, and C) on the 23-day cycle ruler. Place the number on the ruler directly over the first day of the month on the biorhythm chart. Make certain that the horizontal line on the ruler is lined up with the horizontal line on the chart; then draw the *red* rhythm line. Follow the same procedure with ruler for the 28-day cycle, and draw the line in *blue*. Last, take the 33-day ruler and draw a *green* line.

EXAMPLE

|  |  | 23-day Rhythm | 28-day Rhythm | 33-day Rhythm |
|---|---|---|---|---|
| *Step 1:* |  |  |  |  |
| Day of birth: Sept. 16 | Table A. | 19 | 23 | 7 |
| Year of birth: 1939 | Table B. | 15 | 1 | 31 |
|  | Total | 34 | 24 | 38 |
| (If any total is larger than a complete cycle, deduct cycle. If smaller, carry down as is.) |  | 23 | 28 | 33 |
| Basic birth-date figures: |  | 11 | 24 | 5 |

| | | | |
|---|---|---|---|
| Basic birth-date figures: | 11 | 24 | 5 |

Step 2: Select the month and year you
wish to chart, for example: October 1,

| | | | |
|---|---|---|---|
| 1986 | 14 | 23 | 18 |
| | 25 | 47 | 23 |
| | − 23 | − 28 | − (33) |
| again deduct completed cycles (if smaller, carry down as is) . . . . . . . . . | 2 | 19 | 23 |

These final numbers show the exact position of the three rhythms as of October 1, 1986.

People who know the hour of their birth can adjust the position of the rulers so that the cycles start either at the very beginning, the middle, or the end of the space provided for each day on the chart. (See The Importance of the Hour of Birth, in Chapter 3.)

If biorhythm charts are desired for subsequent months, note the rhythm figures shown on the rulers for *the day following* the last day of the month just drawn. If a month ends on the 31st, note the ruler number shown next; if a month ends on the 30th, note the number shown over the 31st because this actually is the first day of the following month.

## INTERPRETATION OF BIORHYTHM CYCLES

A biorhythm chart should always be interpreted in the light of each individual's constitution, age, health, character, and temperament. It is generally recognized that some people are more accident- or error-prone than others, and that some become excited or irritated over trifles, whereas others can endure mental and physical strain with ease. The biorhythm chart, therefore, is a relative picture that has to be studied from all angles.

The periods *above* the horizontal line identify the days of full vitality and efficiency, when a person is at his best and can endure the most.

The periods *below* the horizontal line show the days of reduced efficiency during which the system recuperates and a person is generally not as keen and ambitious and is likely to tire more easily.

During mixed-rhythm periods, for example, when the *red* 23-day physical cycle is high and the *blue* 28-day cycle or the *green* 33-day cycle are low, one can do great things physically but must watch his sensitivity and mental alertness. The reverse position of these cycles indicates soundness in sensitivity or mental alertness, but a physical low period when one may tire more easily.

Critical days in biorhythm are those when the 23-day physical or the 28-day sensitivity cycle passes through the horizontal line, either at the start of a new rhythm or when switching from a high period into a low. There is no reason to fear critical days, or to anticipate an accident or indisposition. These are simply days when a person should be on guard and should avoid situations that might get him involved in trouble.

## TABLE A

### Key Figures for Day of Birth

| | JANUARY | | | | FEBRUARY | | | | MARCH | | |
|---|---|---|---|---|---|---|---|---|---|---|---|
| | 23-Day Cycle | 28-Day Cycle | 33-Day Cycle | | 23-Day Cycle | 28-Day Cycle | 33-Day Cycle | | 23-Day Cycle | 28-Day Cycle | 33-Day Cycle |
| 1 | 1 | 1 | 1 | 1 | 16 | 26 | 3 | 1 | 11 | 26 | 8 |
| 2 | 0 | 0 | 0 | 2 | 15 | 25 | 2 | 2 | 10 | 25 | 7 |
| 3 | 22 | 27 | 32 | 3 | 14 | 24 | 1 | 3 | 9 | 24 | 6 |
| 4 | 21 | 26 | 31 | 4 | 13 | 23 | 0 | 4 | 8 | 23 | 5 |
| 5 | 20 | 25 | 30 | 5 | 12 | 22 | 32 | 5 | 7 | 22 | 4 |
| 6 | 19 | 24 | 29 | 6 | 11 | 21 | 31 | 6 | 6 | 21 | 3 |
| 7 | 18 | 23 | 28 | 7 | 10 | 20 | 30 | 7 | 5 | 20 | 2 |
| 8 | 17 | 22 | 27 | 8 | 9 | 19 | 29 | 8 | 4 | 19 | 1 |
| 9 | 16 | 21 | 26 | 9 | 8 | 18 | 28 | 9 | 3 | 18 | 0 |
| 10 | 15 | 20 | 25 | 10 | 7 | 17 | 27 | 10 | 2 | 17 | 32 |
| 11 | 14 | 19 | 24 | 11 | 6 | 16 | 26 | 11 | 1 | 16 | 31 |
| 12 | 13 | 18 | 23 | 12 | 5 | 15 | 25 | 12 | 0 | 15 | 30 |
| 13 | 12 | 17 | 22 | 13 | 4 | 14 | 24 | 13 | 22 | 14 | 29 |
| 14 | 11 | 16 | 21 | 14 | 3 | 13 | 23 | 14 | 21 | 13 | 28 |
| 15 | 10 | 15 | 20 | 15 | 2 | 12 | 22 | 15 | 20 | 12 | 27 |
| 16 | 9 | 14 | 19 | 16 | 1 | 11 | 21 | 16 | 19 | 11 | 26 |
| 17 | 8 | 13 | 18 | 17 | 0 | 10 | 20 | 17 | 18 | 10 | 25 |
| 18 | 7 | 12 | 17 | 18 | 22 | 9 | 19 | 18 | 17 | 9 | 24 |
| 19 | 6 | 11 | 16 | 19 | 21 | 8 | 18 | 19 | 16 | 8 | 23 |
| 20 | 5 | 10 | 15 | 20 | 20 | 7 | 17 | 20 | 15 | 7 | 22 |
| 21 | 4 | 9 | 14 | 21 | 19 | 6 | 16 | 21 | 14 | 6 | 21 |
| 22 | 3 | 8 | 13 | 22 | 18 | 5 | 15 | 22 | 13 | 5 | 20 |
| 23 | 2 | 7 | 12 | 23 | 17 | 4 | 14 | 23 | 12 | 4 | 19 |
| 24 | 1 | 6 | 11 | 24 | 16 | 3 | 13 | 24 | 11 | 3 | 18 |
| 25 | 0 | 5 | 10 | 25 | 15 | 2 | 12 | 25 | 10 | 2 | 17 |
| 26 | 22 | 4 | 9 | 26 | 14 | 1 | 11 | 26 | 9 | 1 | 16 |
| 27 | 21 | 3 | 8 | 27 | 13 | 0 | 10 | 27 | 8 | 0 | 15 |
| 28 | 20 | 2 | 7 | 28 | 12 | 27 | 9 | 28 | 7 | 27 | 14 |
| 29 | 19 | 1 | 6 | 29 | 11 | 26 | 8 | 29 | 6 | 26 | 13 |
| 30 | 18 | 0 | 5 | | | | | 30 | 5 | 25 | 12 |
| 31 | 17 | 27 | 4 | | | | | 31 | 4 | 24 | 11 |

| | APRIL | | | | MAY | | | | JUNE | | |
|---|---|---|---|---|---|---|---|---|---|---|---|
| | 23-<br>Day<br>Cycle | 28-<br>Day<br>Cycle | 33-<br>Day<br>Cycle | | 23-<br>Day<br>Cycle | 28-<br>Day<br>Cycle | 33-<br>Day<br>Cycle | | 23-<br>Day<br>Cycle | 28-<br>Day<br>Cycle | 33-<br>Day<br>Cycle |
| 1 | 3 | 23 | 10 | 1 | 19 | 21 | 13 | 1 | 11 | 18 | 15 |
| 2 | 2 | 22 | 9 | 2 | 18 | 20 | 12 | 2 | 10 | 17 | 14 |
| 3 | 1 | 21 | 8 | 3 | 17 | 19 | 11 | 3 | 9 | 16 | 13 |
| 4 | 0 | 20 | 7 | 4 | 16 | 18 | 10 | 4 | 8 | 15 | 12 |
| 5 | 22 | 19 | 6 | 5 | 15 | 17 | 9 | 5 | 7 | 14 | 11 |
| 6 | 21 | 18 | 5 | 6 | 14 | 16 | 8 | 6 | 6 | 13 | 10 |
| 7 | 20 | 17 | 4 | 7 | 13 | 15 | 7 | 7 | 5 | 12 | 9 |
| 8 | 19 | 16 | 3 | 8 | 12 | 14 | 6 | 8 | 4 | 11 | 8 |
| 9 | 18 | 15 | 2 | 9 | 11 | 13 | 5 | 9 | 3 | 10 | 7 |
| 10 | 17 | 14 | 1 | 10 | 10 | 12 | 4 | 10 | 2 | 9 | 6 |
| 11 | 16 | 13 | 0 | 11 | 9 | 11 | 3 | 11 | 1 | 8 | 5 |
| 12 | 15 | 12 | 32 | 12 | 8 | 10 | 2 | 12 | 0 | 7 | 4 |
| 13 | 14 | 11 | 31 | 13 | 7 | 9 | 1 | 13 | 22 | 6 | 3 |
| 14 | 13 | 10 | 30 | 14 | 6 | 8 | 0 | 14 | 21 | 5 | 2 |
| 15 | 12 | 9 | 29 | 15 | 5 | 7 | 32 | 15 | 20 | 4 | 1 |
| 16 | 11 | 8 | 28 | 16 | 4 | 6 | 31 | 16 | 19 | 3 | 0 |
| 17 | 0 | 7 | 27 | 17 | 3 | 5 | 30 | 17 | 18 | 2 | 32 |
| 18 | 9 | 6 | 26 | 18 | 2 | 4 | 29 | 18 | 17 | 1 | 31 |
| 19 | 8 | 5 | 25 | 19 | 1 | 3 | 28 | 19 | 16 | 0 | 30 |
| 20 | 7 | 4 | 24 | 20 | 0 | 2 | 27 | 20 | 15 | 27 | 29 |
| 21 | 6 | 3 | 23 | 21 | 22 | 1 | 26 | 21 | 14 | 26 | 28 |
| 22 | 5 | 2 | 22 | 22 | 21 | 0 | 25 | 22 | 13 | 25 | 27 |
| 23 | 4 | 1 | 21 | 23 | 20 | 27 | 24 | 23 | 12 | 24 | 26 |
| 24 | 3 | 0 | 20 | 24 | 19 | 26 | 23 | 24 | 11 | 23 | 25 |
| 25 | 2 | 27 | 19 | 25 | 18 | 25 | 22 | 25 | 10 | 22 | 24 |
| 26 | 1 | 26 | 18 | 26 | 17 | 24 | 21 | 26 | 9 | 21 | 23 |
| 27 | 0 | 25 | 17 | 27 | 16 | 23 | 20 | 27 | 8 | 20 | 22 |
| 28 | 22 | 24 | 16 | 28 | 15 | 22 | 19 | 28 | 7 | 19 | 21 |
| 29 | 21 | 23 | 15 | 29 | 14 | 21 | 18 | 29 | 6 | 18 | 20 |
| 30 | 20 | 22 | 14 | 30 | 13 | 20 | 17 | 30 | 5 | 17 | 19 |
| | | | | 31 | 12 | 19 | 16 | | | | |

## TABLE A — continued
### Key Figures for Day of Birth

|  | JULY 23-Day Cycle | 28-Day Cycle | 33-Day Cycle |  | AUGUST 23-Day Cycle | 28-Day Cycle | 33-Day Cycle |  | SEPTEMBER 23-Day Cycle | 28-Day Cycle | 33-Day Cycle |
|---|---|---|---|---|---|---|---|---|---|---|---|
| 1 | 4 | 16 | 18 | 1 | 19 | 13 | 20 | 1 | 11 | 10 | 22 |
| 2 | 3 | 15 | 17 | 2 | 18 | 12 | 19 | 2 | 10 | 9 | 21 |
| 3 | 2 | 14 | 16 | 3 | 17 | 11 | 18 | 3 | 9 | 8 | 20 |
| 4 | 1 | 13 | 15 | 4 | 16 | 10 | 17 | 4 | 8 | 7 | 19 |
| 5 | 0 | 12 | 14 | 5 | 15 | 9 | 16 | 5 | 7 | 6 | 18 |
| 6 | 22 | 11 | 13 | 6 | 14 | 8 | 15 | 6 | 6 | 5 | 17 |
| 7 | 21 | 10 | 12 | 7 | 13 | 7 | 14 | 7 | 5 | 4 | 16 |
| 8 | 20 | 9 | 11 | 8 | 12 | 6 | 13 | 8 | 4 | 3 | 15 |
| 9 | 19 | 8 | 10 | 9 | 11 | 5 | 12 | 9 | 3 | 2 | 14 |
| 10 | 18 | 7 | 9 | 10 | 10 | 4 | 11 | 10 | 2 | 1 | 13 |
| 11 | 17 | 6 | 8 | 11 | 9 | 3 | 10 | 11 | 1 | 0 | 12 |
| 12 | 16 | 5 | 7 | 12 | 8 | 2 | 9 | 12 | 0 | 27 | 11 |
| 13 | 15 | 4 | 6 | 13 | 7 | 1 | 8 | 13 | 22 | 26 | 10 |
| 14 | 14 | 3 | 5 | 14 | 6 | 0 | 7 | 14 | 21 | 25 | 9 |
| 15 | 13 | 2 | 4 | 15 | 5 | 27 | 6 | 15 | 20 | 24 | 8 |
| 16 | 12 | 1 | 3 | 16 | 4 | 26 | 5 | 16 | 19 | 23 | 7 |
| 17 | 11 | 0 | 2 | 17 | 3 | 25 | 4 | 17 | 18 | 22 | 6 |
| 18 | 10 | 27 | 1 | 18 | 2 | 24 | 3 | 18 | 17 | 21 | 5 |
| 19 | 9 | 26 | 0 | 19 | 1 | 23 | 2 | 19 | 16 | 20 | 4 |
| 20 | 8 | 25 | 32 | 20 | 0 | 22 | 1 | 20 | 15 | 19 | 3 |
| 21 | 7 | 24 | 31 | 21 | 22 | 21 | 0 | 21 | 14 | 18 | 2 |
| 22 | 6 | 23 | 30 | 22 | 21 | 20 | 32 | 22 | 13 | 17 | 1 |
| 23 | 5 | 22 | 29 | 23 | 20 | 19 | 31 | 23 | 12 | 16 | 0 |
| 24 | 4 | 21 | 28 | 24 | 19 | 18 | 30 | 24 | 11 | 15 | 32 |
| 25 | 3 | 20 | 27 | 25 | 18 | 17 | 29 | 25 | 10 | 14 | 31 |
| 26 | 2 | 19 | 26 | 26 | 17 | 16 | 28 | 26 | 9 | 13 | 30 |
| 27 | 1 | 18 | 25 | 27 | 16 | 15 | 27 | 27 | 8 | 12 | 29 |
| 28 | 0 | 17 | 24 | 28 | 15 | 14 | 26 | 28 | 7 | 11 | 28 |
| 29 | 22 | 16 | 23 | 29 | 14 | 13 | 25 | 29 | 6 | 10 | 27 |
| 30 | 21 | 15 | 22 | 30 | 13 | 12 | 24 | 30 | 5 | 9 | 26 |
| 31 | 20 | 14 | 21 | 31 | 12 | 11 | 23 |  |  |  |  |

| | OCTOBER | | | | NOVEMBER | | | | DECEMBER | | |
|---|---|---|---|---|---|---|---|---|---|---|---|
| | 23-Day Cycle | 28-Day Cycle | 33-Day Cycle | | 23-Day Cycle | 28-Day Cycle | 33-Day Cycle | | 23-Day Cycle | 28-Day Cycle | 33-Day Cycle |
| 1 | 4 | 8 | 25 | 1 | 19 | 5 | 27 | 1 | 12 | 3 | 30 |
| 2 | 3 | 7 | 24 | 2 | 18 | 4 | 26 | 2 | 11 | 2 | 29 |
| 3 | 2 | 6 | 23 | 3 | 17 | 3 | 25 | 3 | 10 | 1 | 28 |
| 4 | 1 | 5 | 22 | 4 | 16 | 2 | 24 | 4 | 9 | 0 | 27 |
| 5 | 0 | 4 | 21 | 5 | 15 | 1 | 23 | 5 | 8 | 27 | 26 |
| 6 | 22 | 3 | 20 | 6 | 14 | 0 | 22 | 6 | 7 | 26 | 25 |
| 7 | 21 | 2 | 19 | 7 | 13 | 27 | 21 | 7 | 6 | 25 | 24 |
| 8 | 20 | 1 | 18 | 8 | 12 | 26 | 20 | 8 | 5 | 24 | 23 |
| 9 | 19 | 0 | 17 | 9 | 11 | 25 | 19 | 9 | 4 | 23 | 22 |
| 10 | 18 | 27 | 16 | 10 | 10 | 24 | 18 | 10 | 3 | 22 | 21 |
| 11 | 17 | 26 | 15 | 11 | 9 | 23 | 17 | 11 | 2 | 21 | 20 |
| 12 | 16 | 25 | 14 | 12 | 8 | 22 | 16 | 12 | 1 | 20 | 19 |
| 13 | 15 | 24 | 13 | 13 | 7 | 21 | 15 | 13 | 0 | 19 | 18 |
| 14 | 14 | 23 | 12 | 14 | 6 | 20 | 14 | 14 | 22 | 18 | 17 |
| 15 | 13 | 22 | 11 | 15 | 5 | 19 | 13 | 15 | 21 | 17 | 16 |
| 16 | 12 | 21 | 10 | 16 | 4 | 18 | 12 | 16 | 20 | 16 | 15 |
| 17 | 11 | 20 | 9 | 17 | 3 | 17 | 11 | 17 | 19 | 15 | 14 |
| 18 | 10 | 19 | 8 | 18 | 2 | 16 | 10 | 18 | 18 | 14 | 13 |
| 19 | 9 | 18 | 7 | 19 | 1 | 15 | 9 | 19 | 17 | 13 | 12 |
| 20 | 8 | 17 | 6 | 20 | 0 | 14 | 8 | 20 | 16 | 12 | 11 |
| 21 | 7 | 16 | 5 | 21 | 22 | 13 | 7 | 21 | 15 | 11 | 10 |
| 22 | 6 | 15 | 4 | 22 | 21 | 12 | 6 | 22 | 14 | 10 | 9 |
| 23 | 5 | 14 | 3 | 23 | 20 | 11 | 5 | 23 | 13 | 9 | 8 |
| 24 | 4 | 13 | 2 | 24 | 19 | 10 | 4 | 24 | 12 | 8 | 7 |
| 25 | 3 | 12 | 1 | 25 | 18 | 9 | 3 | 25 | 11 | 7 | 6 |
| 26 | 2 | 11 | 0 | 26 | 17 | 8 | 2 | 26 | 10 | 6 | 5 |
| 27 | 1 | 10 | 32 | 27 | 16 | 7 | 1 | 27 | 9 | 5 | 4 |
| 28 | 0 | 9 | 31 | 28 | 15 | 6 | 0 | 28 | 8 | 4 | 3 |
| 29 | 22 | 8 | 30 | 29 | 14 | 5 | 32 | 29 | 7 | 3 | 2 |
| 30 | 21 | 7 | 29 | 30 | 13 | 4 | 31 | 30 | 6 | 2 | 1 |
| 31 | 20 | 6 | 28 | | | | | 31 | 5 | 1 | 0 |

## TABLE B

### Key Figures for Year of Birth

* LY indicates leap years.
** 1900 was not a leap year.
People born in a leap year between March and December must deduct 1 day from the value shown in each cycle.
For those born in a leap year between January 1 and February 29, the values shown in this chart remain as they are.

| | 23-Day Cycle | 28-Day Cycle | 33-Day Cycle | | 23-Day Cycle | 28-Day Cycle | 33-Day Cycle |
|---|---|---|---|---|---|---|---|
| 1887 | 9 | 9 | 15 | 1920 LY | 9 | 25 | 8 |
| 1888 LY | 12 | 8 | 13 | 1921 | 11 | 23 | 5 |
| 1889 | 14 | 6 | 10 | 1922 | 14 | 22 | 3 |
| 1890 | 17 | 5 | 8 | 1923 | 17 | 21 | 1 |
| 1891 | 20 | 4 | 6 | 1924 LY | 20 | 20 | 32 |
| 1892 LY | 0 | 3 | 4 | 1925 | 22 | 18 | 29 |
| 1893 | 2 | 1 | 1 | 1926 | 2 | 17 | 27 |
| 1894 | 5 | 0 | 32 | 1927 | 5 | 16 | 25 |
| 1895 | 8 | 27 | 30 | 1928 LY | 8 | 15 | 23 |
| 1896 LY | 11 | 26 | 28 | 1929 | 10 | 13 | 20 |
| 1897 | 13 | 24 | 25 | 1930 | 13 | 12 | 18 |
| 1898 | 16 | 23 | 23 | 1931 | 16 | 11 | 16 |
| 1899 | 19 | 22 | 21 | 1932 LY | 19 | 10 | 14 |
| 1900** | 22 | 21 | 19 | 1933 | 21 | 8 | 11 |
| 1901 | 2 | 20 | 17 | 1934 | 1 | 7 | 9 |
| 1902 | 5 | 19 | 15 | 1935 | 4 | 6 | 7 |
| 1903 | 8 | 18 | 13 | 1936 LY | 7 | 5 | 5 |
| 1904 LY | 11 | 17 | 11 | 1937 | 9 | 3 | 2 |
| 1905 | 13 | 15 | 8 | 1938 | 12 | 2 | 0 |
| 1906 | 16 | 14 | 6 | 1939 | 15 | 1 | 31 |
| 1907 | 19 | 13 | 4 | 1940 LY | 18 | 0 | 29 |
| 1908 LY | 22 | 12 | 2 | 1941 | 20 | 26 | 26 |
| 1909 | 1 | 10 | 32 | 1942 | 0 | 25 | 24 |
| 1910 | 4 | 9 | 30 | 1943 | 3 | 24 | 22 |
| 1911 | 7 | 8 | 28 | 1944 LY | 6 | 23 | 20 |
| 1912 LY | 10 | 7 | 26 | 1945 | 8 | 21 | 17 |
| 1913 | 12 | 5 | 23 | 1946 | 11 | 20 | 15 |
| 1914 | 15 | 4 | 21 | 1947 | 14 | 19 | 13 |
| 1915 | 18 | 3 | 19 | 1948 LY | 17 | 18 | 11 |
| 1916 LY | 21 | 2 | 17 | 1949 | 19 | 16 | 8 |
| 1917 | 0 | 0 | 14 | 1950 | 22 | 15 | 6 |
| 1918 | 3 | 27 | 12 | 1951 | 2 | 14 | 4 |
| 1919 | 6 | 26 | 10 | 1952 LY | 5 | 13 | 2 |

\* LY indicates leap years.
\*\* 1900 was not a leap year.
People born in a leap year between March and December must deduct 1 day from the value shown in each cycle.
For those born in a leap year between January 1 and February 29, the values shown in this chart remain as they are.

| | 23-Day Cycle | 28-Day Cycle | 33-Day Cycle | | 23-Day Cycle | 28-Day Cycle | 33-Day Cycle |
|---|---|---|---|---|---|---|---|
| 1953 | 7 | 11 | 32 | 1977 | 4 | 9 | 11 |
| 1954 | 10 | 10 | 30 | 1978 | 7 | 8 | 9 |
| 1955 | 13 | 9 | 28 | 1979 | 10 | 7 | 7 |
| 1956 LY | 16 | 8 | 26 | 1980 LY | 13 | 6 | 5 |
| 1957 | 18 | 6 | 23 | 1981 | 15 | 4 | 2 |
| 1958 | 21 | 5 | 21 | 1982 | 18 | 3 | 0 |
| 1959 | 1 | 4 | 19 | 1983 | 21 | 2 | 31 |
| 1960 LY | 4 | 3 | 17 | 1984 LY | 1 | 1 | 29 |
| 1961 | 6 | 1 | 14 | 1985 | 3 | 27 | 26 |
| 1962 | 9 | 0 | 12 | 1986 | 6 | 26 | 24 |
| 1963 | 12 | 27 | 10 | 1987 | 9 | 25 | 22 |
| 1964 LY | 15 | 26 | 8 | 1988 LY | 12 | 24 | 20 |
| 1965 | 17 | 24 | 5 | 1989 | 14 | 22 | 17 |
| 1966 | 20 | 23 | 3 | 1990 | 17 | 21 | 15 |
| 1967 | 0 | 22 | 1 | 1991 | 20 | 20 | 13 |
| 1968 LY | 3 | 21 | 32 | 1992 LY | 0 | 19 | 11 |
| 1969 | 5 | 19 | 29 | 1993 | 2 | 17 | 8 |
| 1970 | 8 | 18 | 27 | 1994 | 5 | 16 | 6 |
| 1971 | 11 | 17 | 25 | 1995 | 8 | 15 | 4 |
| 1972 LY | 14 | 16 | 23 | 1996 LY | 11 | 14 | 2 |
| 1973 | 16 | 14 | 20 | 1997 | 13 | 12 | 32 |
| 1974 | 19 | 13 | 18 | 1998 | 16 | 11 | 30 |
| 1975 | 22 | 12 | 16 | 1999 | 19 | 10 | 28 |
| 1976 LY | 2 | 11 | 14 | 2000 LY | 22 | 9 | 26 |

## TABLE C
### Biorhythm Condition Testing Values
(Calculated as of the first of each month)

| 1982 | | | 1983 | | | 1984 LY | | |
|---|---|---|---|---|---|---|---|---|
| Jan. | 5 | 25 | 0 | Jan. | 2 | 26 | 2 | Jan. | 22 | 27 | 4 |

| | 1982 | | | | 1983 | | | | 1984 LY | | |
|------|----|----|----|------|----|----|----|------|----|----|----|
| Jan. | 5 | 25 | 0 | Jan. | 2 | 26 | 2 | Jan. | 22 | 27 | 4 |
| Feb. | 13 | 0 | 31 | Feb. | 10 | 1 | 0 | Feb. | 7 | 2 | 2 |
| Mar. | 18 | 0 | 26 | Mar. | 15 | 1 | 28 | Mar. | 13 | 3 | 31 |
| Apr. | 3 | 3 | 24 | Apr. | 0 | 4 | 26 | Apr. | 21 | 6 | 29 |
| May | 10 | 5 | 21 | May | 7 | 6 | 23 | May | 5 | 8 | 26 |
| June | 18 | 8 | 19 | June | 15 | 9 | 21 | June | 13 | 11 | 24 |
| July | 2 | 10 | 16 | July | 22 | 11 | 18 | July | 20 | 13 | 21 |
| Aug. | 10 | 13 | 14 | Aug. | 7 | 14 | 16 | Aug. | 5 | 16 | 19 |
| Sept. | 18 | 16 | 12 | Sept. | 15 | 17 | 14 | Sept. | 13 | 19 | 17 |
| Oct. | 2 | 18 | 9 | Oct. | 22 | 19 | 11 | Oct. | 20 | 21 | 14 |
| Nov. | 10 | 21 | 7 | Nov. | 7 | 22 | 9 | Nov. | 5 | 24 | 12 |
| Dec. | 17 | 23 | 4 | Dec. | 14 | 24 | 6 | Dec. | 12 | 26 | 9 |

| | 1985 | | | | 1986 | | | | 1987 | | |
|------|----|----|----|------|----|----|----|------|----|----|----|
| Jan. | 20 | 1 | 7 | Jan. | 17 | 2 | 9 | Jan. | 14 | 3 | 11 |
| Feb. | 5 | 4 | 5 | Feb. | 2 | 5 | 7 | Feb. | 22 | 6 | 9 |
| Mar. | 10 | 4 | 0 | Mar. | 7 | 5 | 2 | Mar. | 4 | 6 | 4 |
| Apr. | 18 | 7 | 31 | Apr. | 15 | 8 | 0 | Apr. | 12 | 9 | 2 |
| May | 2 | 9 | 28 | May | 22 | 10 | 30 | May | 19 | 11 | 32 |
| June | 10 | 12 | 26 | June | 7 | 13 | 28 | June | 4 | 14 | 30 |
| July | 17 | 14 | 23 | July | 14 | 15 | 25 | July | 11 | 16 | 27 |
| Aug. | 2 | 17 | 21 | Aug. | 22 | 18 | 23 | Aug. | 19 | 19 | 25 |
| Sept. | 10 | 20 | 19 | Sept. | 7 | 21 | 21 | Sept. | 4 | 22 | 23 |
| Oct. | 17 | 22 | 16 | Oct. | 14 | 23 | 18 | Oct. | 11 | 24 | 20 |
| Nov. | 2 | 25 | 14 | Nov. | 22 | 26 | 16 | Nov. | 19 | 27 | 18 |
| Dec. | 9 | 27 | 11 | Dec. | 6 | 0 | 13 | Dec. | 3 | 1 | 15 |

| | 1988 LY | | | | 1989 | | | | 1990 | | |
|------|----|----|----|------|----|----|----|------|----|----|----|
| Jan. | 11 | 4 | 13 | Jan. | 9 | 6 | 16 | Jan. | 6 | 7 | 18 |
| Feb. | 19 | 7 | 11 | Feb. | 17 | 9 | 14 | Feb. | 14 | 10 | 16 |
| Mar. | 2 | 8 | 7 | Mar. | 22 | 9 | 9 | Mar. | 19 | 10 | 11 |
| Apr. | 10 | 11 | 5 | Apr. | 7 | 12 | 7 | Apr. | 4 | 13 | 9 |
| May | 17 | 13 | 2 | May | 14 | 14 | 4 | May | 11 | 15 | 6 |
| June | 2 | 16 | 0 | June | 22 | 17 | 2 | June | 19 | 18 | 4 |
| July | 9 | 18 | 30 | July | 6 | 19 | 32 | July | 3 | 20 | 1 |
| Aug. | 17 | 21 | 28 | Aug. | 14 | 22 | 30 | Aug. | 11 | 23 | 32 |
| Sept. | 2 | 24 | 26 | Sept. | 22 | 25 | 28 | Sept. | 19 | 26 | 30 |
| Oct. | 9 | 26 | 23 | Oct. | 6 | 27 | 25 | Oct. | 3 | 0 | 27 |
| Nov. | 17 | 1 | 21 | Nov. | 14 | 2 | 23 | Nov. | 11 | 3 | 25 |
| Dec. | 1 | 3 | 18 | Dec. | 21 | 4 | 20 | Dec. | 18 | 5 | 22 |

# TABLE C—continued

| | 1991 | | | | 1992 LY | | | | 1993 | | |
|------|----|----|----|------|----|----|----|------|----|----|----|
| Jan. | 3 | 8 | 20 | Jan. | 0 | 9 | 22 | Jan. | 21 | 11 | 25 |
| Feb. | 11 | 11 | 18 | Feb. | 8 | 12 | 20 | Feb. | 6 | 14 | 23 |
| Mar. | 16 | 11 | 13 | Mar. | 14 | 13 | 16 | Mar. | 11 | 14 | 18 |
| Apr. | 1 | 14 | 11 | Apr. | 22 | 16 | 14 | Apr. | 19 | 17 | 16 |
| May | 8 | 16 | 8 | May | 6 | 18 | 11 | May | 3 | 19 | 13 |
| June | 16 | 19 | 6 | June | 14 | 21 | 9 | June | 11 | 22 | 11 |
| July | 0 | 21 | 3 | July | 21 | 23 | 6 | July | 18 | 24 | 8 |
| Aug. | 8 | 24 | 1 | Aug. | 6 | 26 | 4 | Aug. | 3 | 27 | 6 |
| Sept. | 16 | 27 | 32 | Sept. | 14 | 1 | 2 | Sept. | 11 | 2 | 4 |
| Oct. | 0 | 1 | 29 | Oct. | 21 | 3 | 32 | Oct. | 18 | 4 | 1 |
| Nov. | 8 | 4 | 27 | Nov. | 6 | 6 | 30 | Nov. | 3 | 7 | 32 |
| Dec. | 15 | 6 | 24 | Dec. | 13 | 8 | 27 | Dec. | 10 | 9 | 29 |

| | 1994 | | | | 1995 | | | | 1996 LY | | |
|------|----|----|----|------|----|----|----|------|----|----|----|
| Jan. | 18 | 12 | 27 | Jan. | 15 | 13 | 29 | Jan. | 12 | 14 | 31 |
| Feb. | 3 | 15 | 25 | Feb. | 0 | 16 | 27 | Feb. | 20 | 17 | 29 |
| Mar. | 8 | 15 | 20 | Mar. | 5 | 16 | 22 | Mar. | 3 | 18 | 25 |
| Apr. | 16 | 18 | 18 | Apr. | 13 | 19 | 20 | Apr. | 11 | 21 | 23 |
| May | 0 | 20 | 15 | May | 20 | 21 | 17 | May | 18 | 23 | 20 |
| June | 8 | 23 | 13 | June | 5 | 24 | 15 | June | 3 | 26 | 18 |
| July | 15 | 25 | 10 | July | 12 | 26 | 12 | July | 10 | 0 | 15 |
| Aug. | 0 | 0 | 8 | Aug. | 20 | 1 | 10 | Aug. | 18 | 3 | 13 |
| Sept. | 8 | 3 | 6 | Sept. | 5 | 4 | 8 | Sept. | 3 | 6 | 11 |
| Oct. | 15 | 5 | 3 | Oct. | 12 | 6 | 5 | Oct. | 10 | 8 | 8 |
| Nov. | 0 | 8 | 1 | Nov. | 20 | 9 | 3 | Nov. | 18 | 11 | 6 |
| Dec. | 7 | 10 | 31 | Dec. | 4 | 11 | 0 | Dec. | 2 | 13 | 3 |

| | 1997 | | | | 1998 | | | | 1999 | | |
|------|----|----|----|------|----|----|----|------|----|----|----|
| Jan. | 10 | 16 | 1 | Jan. | 7 | 17 | 3 | Jan. | 4 | 18 | 5 |
| Feb. | 18 | 19 | 32 | Feb. | 15 | 20 | 1 | Feb. | 12 | 21 | 3 |
| Mar. | 0 | 19 | 27 | Mar. | 20 | 20 | 29 | Mar. | 17 | 21 | 31 |
| Apr. | 8 | 22 | 25 | Apr. | 5 | 23 | 27 | Apr. | 2 | 24 | 29 |
| May | 15 | 24 | 22 | May | 12 | 25 | 24 | May | 9 | 26 | 26 |
| June | 0 | 27 | 20 | June | 20 | 0 | 22 | June | 17 | 1 | 24 |
| July | 7 | 1 | 17 | July | 4 | 2 | 19 | July | 1 | 3 | 21 |
| Aug. | 15 | 4 | 15 | Aug. | 12 | 5 | 17 | Aug. | 9 | 6 | 19 |
| Sept. | 0 | 7 | 13 | Sept. | 20 | 8 | 15 | Sept. | 17 | 9 | 17 |
| Oct. | 7 | 9 | 10 | Oct. | 4 | 10 | 12 | Oct. | 1 | 11 | 14 |
| Nov. | 15 | 12 | 8 | Nov. | 12 | 13 | 10 | Nov. | 9 | 14 | 12 |
| Dec. | 22 | 14 | 5 | Dec. | 19 | 15 | 7 | Dec. | 16 | 16 | 9 |

## TABLE C—continued

|  | 2000 LY |  |  |  | 2001 |  |  |  | 2002 |  |  |
|---|---|---|---|---|---|---|---|---|---|---|---|
| Jan. | 1 | 19 | 7 | Jan. | 22 | 21 | 10 | Jan. | 19 | 22 | 12 |
| Feb. | 9 | 22 | 5 | Feb. | 7 | 24 | 8 | Feb. | 4 | 25 | 10 |
| Mar. | 15 | 23 | 1 | Mar. | 12 | 24 | 3 | Mar. | 9 | 25 | 5 |
| Apr. | 0 | 26 | 32 | Apr. | 20 | 27 | 1 | Apr. | 17 | 0 | 3 |
| May | 7 | 0 | 29 | May | 4 | 1 | 31 | May | 1 | 2 | 0 |
| June | 15 | 3 | 27 | June | 12 | 4 | 29 | June | 9 | 5 | 31 |
| July | 22 | 5 | 24 | July | 19 | 6 | 26 | July | 16 | 7 | 28 |
| Aug. | 7 | 8 | 22 | Aug. | 4 | 9 | 24 | Aug. | 1 | 10 | 26 |
| Sept. | 15 | 11 | 20 | Sept. | 12 | 12 | 22 | Sept. | 9 | 13 | 24 |
| Oct. | 22 | 13 | 17 | Oct. | 19 | 14 | 19 | Oct. | 16 | 15 | 21 |
| Nov. | 7 | 16 | 15 | Nov. | 4 | 17 | 17 | Nov. | 1 | 18 | 19 |
| Dec. | 14 | 18 | 12 | Dec. | 11 | 19 | 14 | Dec. | 8 | 20 | 16 |

|  | 2003 |  |  |  | 2004 LY |  |  |  | 2005 |  |  |
|---|---|---|---|---|---|---|---|---|---|---|---|
| Jan. | 16 | 23 | 14 | Jan. | 13 | 24 | 16 | Jan. | 11 | 26 | 19 |
| Feb. | 1 | 26 | 12 | Feb. | 21 | 27 | 14 | Feb. | 19 | 1 | 17 |
| Mar. | 6 | 26 | 7 | Mar. | 4 | 0 | 10 | Mar. | 1 | 1 | 12 |
| Apr. | 14 | 1 | 5 | Apr. | 12 | 3 | 8 | Apr. | 9 | 4 | 10 |
| May | 21 | 3 | 2 | May | 19 | 5 | 5 | May | 16 | 6 | 7 |
| June | 6 | 6 | 0 | June | 4 | 8 | 3 | June | 1 | 9 | 5 |
| July | 13 | 8 | 30 | July | 11 | 10 | 0 | July | 8 | 11 | 2 |
| Aug. | 21 | 11 | 28 | Aug. | 19 | 13 | 31 | Aug. | 16 | 14 | 0 |
| Sept. | 6 | 14 | 26 | Sept. | 4 | 16 | 29 | Sept. | 1 | 17 | 31 |
| Oct. | 13 | 16 | 23 | Oct. | 11 | 18 | 26 | Oct. | 8 | 19 | 28 |
| Nov. | 21 | 19 | 21 | Nov. | 19 | 21 | 24 | Nov. | 16 | 22 | 26 |
| Dec. | 5 | 21 | 18 | Dec. | 3 | 23 | 21 | Dec. | 0 | 24 | 23 |

|  | 2006 |  |  |  | 2007 |  |  |  | 2008 LY |  |  |
|---|---|---|---|---|---|---|---|---|---|---|---|
| Jan. | 8 | 27 | 21 | Jan. | 5 | 0 | 23 | Jan. | 2 | 1 | 25 |
| Feb. | 16 | 2 | 19 | Feb. | 13 | 3 | 21 | Feb. | 10 | 4 | 23 |
| Mar. | 21 | 2 | 14 | Mar. | 18 | 3 | 16 | Mar. | 16 | 5 | 19 |
| Apr. | 6 | 5 | 12 | Apr. | 3 | 6 | 14 | Apr. | 1 | 8 | 17 |
| May | 13 | 7 | 9 | May | 10 | 8 | 11 | May | 8 | 10 | 14 |
| June | 21 | 10 | 7 | June | 18 | 11 | 9 | June | 16 | 13 | 12 |
| July | 5 | 12 | 4 | July | 2 | 13 | 6 | July | 0 | 15 | 9 |
| Aug. | 13 | 15 | 2 | Aug. | 10 | 16 | 4 | Aug. | 8 | 18 | 7 |
| Sept. | 21 | 18 | 0 | Sept. | 18 | 19 | 2 | Sept. | 16 | 21 | 5 |
| Oct. | 5 | 20 | 30 | Oct. | 2 | 21 | 32 | Oct. | 0 | 23 | 2 |
| Nov. | 13 | 23 | 28 | Nov. | 10 | 24 | 30 | Nov. | 8 | 26 | 0 |
| Dec. | 20 | 25 | 25 | Dec. | 17 | 26 | 27 | Dec. | 15 | 0 | 30 |

# BIBLIOGRAPHY

ANDERSON, RUSSELL K. *Biorhythm—Man's Timing Mechanism.* American Society of Safety Engineers, Park Ridge, Ill.

BIO-CALENDAR, INC., P. O. Box 66509, St. Petersburg Beach, FL 33736.

BOCHOW, REINHOLD. *Der Unfall im landwirtschaftlichen Betrieb.* Dissertation presented at Humboldt University in Berlin, 1954. Wissenschaftliche Zeitschrift der Humboldt University zu Berlin, Jahrgang IV, 1954–55.

BRADY, TIM, Major USAF. *Biorhythm What? TAC Attack.* USAF Tactical Air Command, Langley Air Force Base, March, 1972.

DREISKE, PAUL. "Are There Strange Forces in Our Lives?" *Family Safety,* 1972. National Safety Council, Chicago.

FLIESS, WILHELM, M.D. *Vom Leben und vom Tod.* A collection of lectures in biology relating to the 23-day and 28-day rhythms, with an interesting analysis of the inheritance of left-handedness. Eugen Diederichs, Jena, 1909. Second edition, 1914.

———. *Das Jahr im Lebendigen.* The origin of the rhythms in life. Eugen Diederichs, Jena, 1918. Second edition, 1924.

*133*

―――. *Der Ablauf des Lebens.* A 564-page documentation explaining the discovery of the 23-day and 28-day rhythms in man. Franz Deuticke, Leipzig-Vienna, 1906. Second edition, 1923.

―――. *Zur Periodenlehre.* A collection of lectures. Ebenda Verlag, Leipzig, 1925.

FRUEH, HANS. *Von der Periodenlehre zur Biorhythmenlehre.* Wegweiser-Verlag, Zurich-Leipzig, 1939–42.

―――. *Rhythmenpraxis.* Verlag H. R. Frueh, Bassersdorf, Zurich, 1943.

―――. *Kraft, Gesundheit und Leistung—Der Rhythmus der Kraefte im Menschen.* Selbstverlag, Bassersdorf, 1946.

―――. *Deine Leistungskurve.* A collection of lectures and documentation. Verlag H. R. Frueh, Bassersdorf, Zurich, 1953.

―――. *Triumph der Lebensrhythmen.* Lebensweiser-Verlag, Buedingen-Gettenbach, 1954.

GROSS, HUGO MAX. *Biorhythmik, Das Auf und Ab Unserer Lebenskraft.* Verlag Hermann Bauer, Freiburg im Bresgau, 1959.

HALBERG, FRANZ. *Physiologic 24-Hour Periodicity;* etc. Zeitschrift fuer Vitamin—Hormon—and Fermentforschung, Band X, Heft 3/4, pages 278–84, 1959.

HERBART, JOHANN FRIEDRICH. *Textbook on Psychology.* International Education Series #18. G. Hartenstein, Leipzig, 1850–52.

KURTH, HANNS. *Mit Biorhythmik lebt es sich leichter.* Albert-Mueller-Verlag, Ruschlikon, Switzerland.

LUCE, GAY GAER. *Biological Rhythms in Human and Animal Physiology.* Dover Publications, Inc., New York.

PFEFFER, WILHELM. *Pflanzenphysiologie.* W. Engelman, Leipzig.

————. *Schlafbewegung der Blattorgane.* B. C. Teubner, Leipzig, 1917.

ROSSIER, ANT. *Traité de Rythmologie.* La prévision scientifique de la destinée. Editions Ère Nouvelle, Lausanne.

SCHATTEN, GERALD, and HEIDE SCHATTEN. "The Energetic Egg," *The Sciences*, October, 1983.

SCHLIEPER, HANS, M.D. *Der Rhythmus des Lebendigen.* A review of the discovery of regulated rhythms by Wilhelm Fliess, M.D. Eugen Diederichs, Jena, 1909.

————. *Das Jahr im Raum.* Eugen Diederichs, Jena.

SCHWING, HANS. *Ueber Biorhythmen und deren technische Anwendung.* Dissertation presented at the Swiss Federal Institute of Technology. A. G. Gebr. Leemann & Co., 1939.

SUGGS, TOMMY. *Behind the Scenes,* York Training Secrets, *Biorhythm.* Strength and Health Publishing Co., York, Pa., July, 1967.

SWOBODA, DR. HERMANN. *Die Perioden des menschlichen Lebens in ihrer psychologischen und biologischen Bedeutung.* Franz Deuticke, Leipzig and Vienna, 1904.

————. *Studien zur Grundlegung der Psychologie.* Franz Deuticke, Leipzig and Vienna, 1905.

————. *Die kritischen Tage des Menschen in ihre Berechnung mit dem Periodenschieber.* Franz Deuticke, Leipzig and Vienna, 1909.

————. *Das Siebenjahn.* A 576-page documentation tracing rhythmical relationship through generations. Orion-Verlag, Vienna and Leipzig, 1917.

————. *Die Bedeutung des Siebenjahn Rhythmus fuer die menschliche Vererbung.* Industria Tipografica Fiorentina, Firenze, 1954.

*135*

TOPE, O. *Biorhythmische Einfluesse und ihre Auswirkung in Fuhrparkbetrieben.* Sonderdruck: Staedtehygiene 9/1956, Hannover.

WALDECK, HANS. *Der Rhythmus deines Blutes. Die Biorhythmik als Naturgesetz.* Lebensweiser-Verlag, A. G., Buedingen, 1952.

————. *Dein Bluttakt ist dein Schicksal.* The influence of the rhythm of the blood on man's fate. Lebensweiser-Verlag, A. G., Buedingen.

————. *Ebbe und Flut im Menschen.* The tides in man. Lebensweiser-Verlag, A. G., Buedingen.

WENT, FRITZ W. *Ecological Implications of the Autonomous 24-Hour Rhythm in Plants.* Annals of the New York Academy of Sciences, Vol. 98, Art. 4, page 866.

WERNLI, HANS. *Biorhythm, A Scientific Exploration into the Life Cycles of the Individual.*

*136*

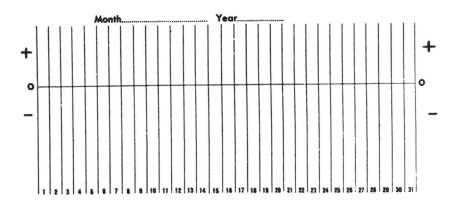

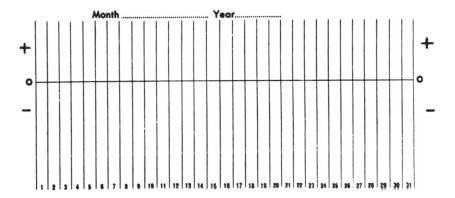

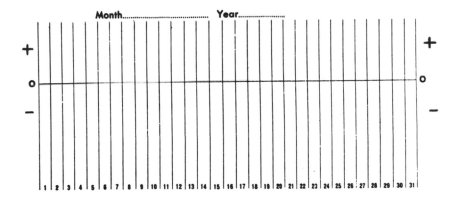

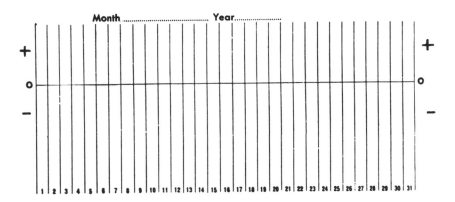

Month.................................... Year.....................

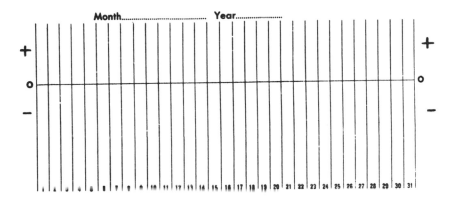

Month.................................... Year.....................

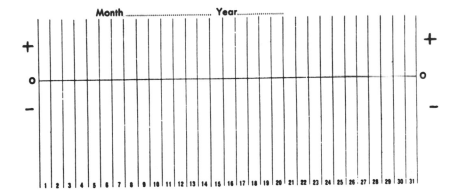

Month.................................... Year.....................

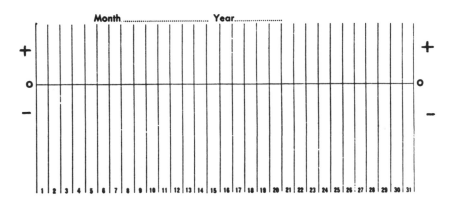

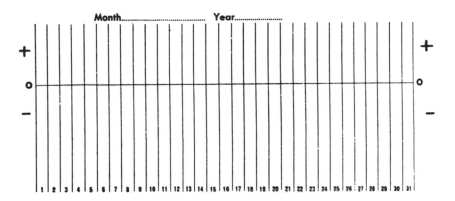

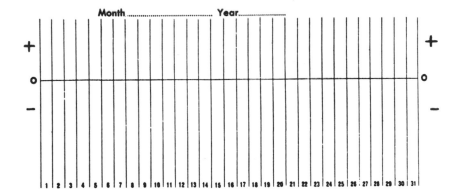

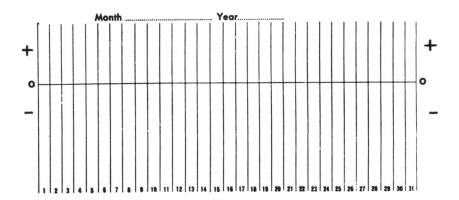

Month.................................... Year....................

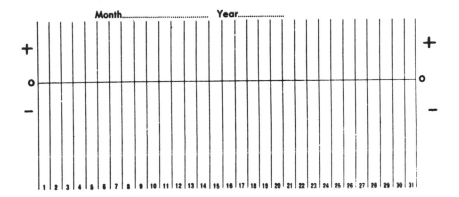

Month.................................... Year....................

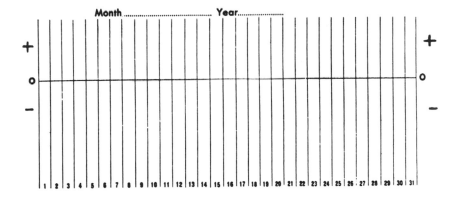

Month.................................... Year....................

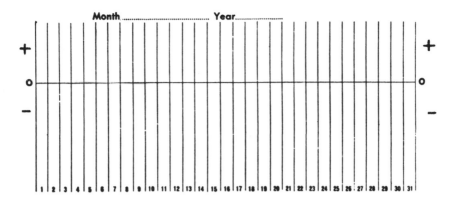

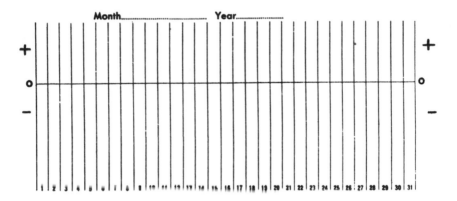

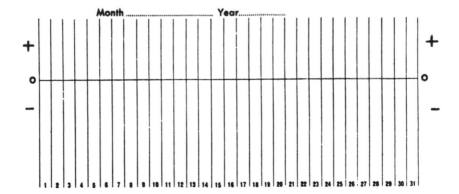

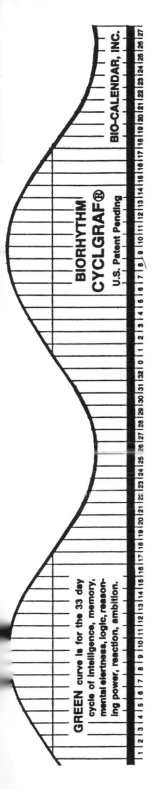

GREEN curve is for the 33 day cycle of Intelligence, memory, mental alertness, logic, reasoning power, reaction, ambition.

BIORHYTHM CYCLGRAF®

U.S. Patent Pending

BIO-CALENDAR, INC.

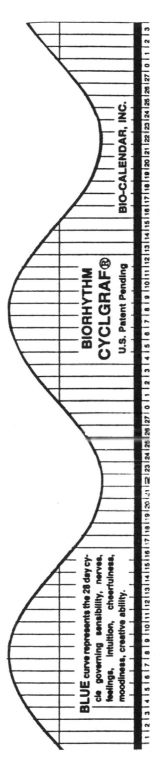

BLUE curve represents the 28 day cycle governing sensibility, nerves, feelings, intuition, cheerfulness, moodiness, creative ability.

BIORHYTHM CYCLGRAF®

U.S. Patent Pending

BIO-CALENDAR, INC.

RED curve represents the 23 day cycle of physical strength, endurance, energy, resistance, confidence.

BIORHYTHM CYCLGRAF®

U.S. Patent Pending

BIO-CALENDAR, INC.